WALKING IN THE SALZKAMMERGUT: THE AUSTRIAN LAKE DISTRICT

About the Author

Rudolf Abraham (www.rudolfabraham.co.uk) is an award-winning travel writer and photographer specialising in Central and Eastern Europe. He is the author of a dozen books and has contributed to many more, and his work is published widely in magazines.

Other Cicerone guides by the author

St Oswald's and St Cuthbert's Way
The Islands of Croatia
The Mountains of Montenegro
The Peaks of the Balkans Trail
Torres del Paine
Walks and Treks in Croatia

Updates to this guide

While every effort is made by our authors to ensure the accuracy of guidebooks as they go to print, changes can occur during the lifetime of an edition. This guidebook was researched and written before the COVID-19 pandemic. While we are not aware of any significant changes to routes or facilities at the time of printing, it is likely that the current situation will give rise to more changes than would usually be expected. Any updates that we know of will be on the Cicerone website (www.cicerone.co.uk/996/updates), so please check before planning your trip. We also advise that you check information about such things as transport, accommodation and shops locally. Even rights of way can be altered over time.

We are always grateful for information about any discrepancies between a guidebook and the facts on the ground, sent by email to updates@cicerone.co.uk or by post to Juniper House, Murley Moss, Oxenholme Road, Kendal, LA9 7RL.

Register your book: to sign up to receive free updates, special offers and GPX files where available, register your book at www.cicerone.co.uk.

WALKING IN THE SALZKAMMERGUT: THE AUSTRIAN LAKE DISTRICT

30 WALKS IN SALZBURG'S LAKES AND MOUNTAINS, INCLUDING THE DACHSTEIN

by Rudolf Abraham

JUNIPER HOUSE, MURLEY MOSS,
OXENHOLME ROAD, KENDAL, CUMBRIA LA9 7RL
www.cicerone.co.uk

© Rudolf Abraham 2021
First edition 2021
ISBN: 978 1 85284 996 2

Printed in Singapore by KHL using responsibly sourced paper
A catalogue record for this book is available from the British Library.
All photographs are by the author unless otherwise stated.

Route mapping by Lovell Johns www.lovelljohns.com
Contains OpenStreetMap.org data © OpenStreetMap
contributors, CC-BY-SA. NASA relief data courtesy of ESRI

For my daughter Tamara, who was with me every step of the way.

Acknowledgements

I would like to thank the following people for their support and enthusiasm while I worked on this guide: Ernst Kammerer and Theresa Schwaiger at Tourismusverband Ausseerland; Thomas Möslinger at Wolfgangsee Tourismus; Gerhard Spengler at Tourismusverband Traunsee-Almtal in Ebensee; Stephan Köhl at Tourismusverband Bad Ischl; Petra Wieder at Salzkammergut Tourismus Marketing; Melanie Grasberger at Tourismusverband Traunsee-Almtal Gmunden; Stefanie Wallner at Ferienregion Dachstein Salzkammergut in Bad Goisern; Renate Kritzinger at Wiesberghaus; Martina Jamnig and Eleanor Moody of the Austrian National Tourist Office in London; and Ulrich Teitz at Deutsche Bahn. Last but not least, I would like to thank my daughter Tamara, who between the age of seven and nine made half a dozen trips to Austria with me while I was writing this book, and proved herself the best hiking company anyone could ever ask for.

Front cover: View across Vorderer Gosausee (Walk 28)

CONTENTS

Note on mapping

The route maps in this guide are derived from publicly available data, databases and crowd-sourced data. As such they have not been through the detailed checking procedures that would generally be applied to a published map from an official mapping agency. We have reviewed them closely in the light of local knowledge as part of the preparation of this guide – however, for more information consult the sheet map(s) recommended in this guide.

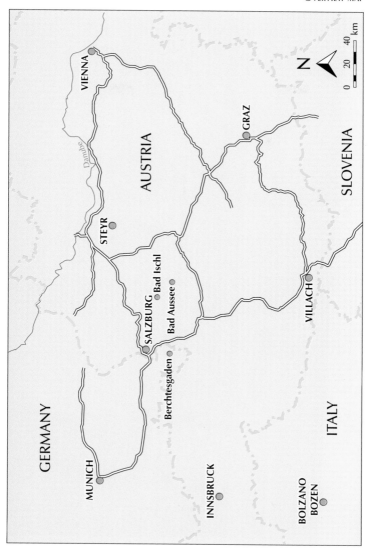

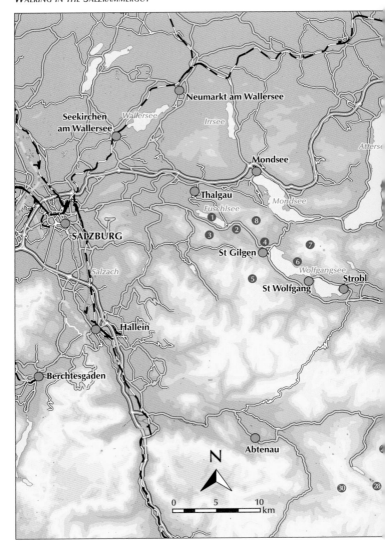

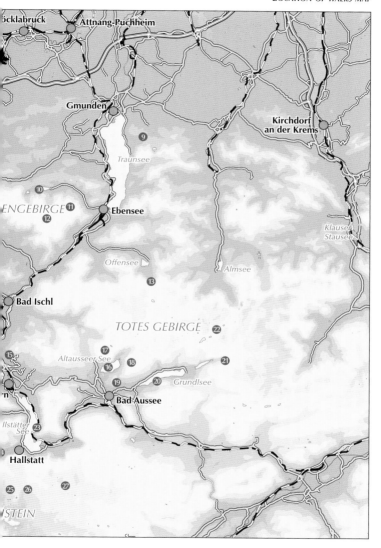

Symbols used on route maps

〜	route
- 〜 -	alternative route
Ⓢ	start point
Ⓕ	finish point
⑤Ⓕ	start/finish point
Ⓕ	alternative finish point
>	route direction
☁	glacier
	woodland
	urban areas
	international border
⚓	ferry
- - - ·	ferry route
▬■▬	station/railway
■	bus stop
P	parking
🚠	cable car
▲	peak
◗	cave
⬆	hut with food and accommodation
⬒	hut with food (no accommodation)
⬚	refreshments
■	building
╪†	church or chapel/cross
⊓	castle
≍	pass
•	water feature
✳	viewpoint

Relief
in metres

3000 and above	
2800–3000	
2600–2800	
2400–2600	
2200–2400	
2000–2200	
1800–2000	
1600–1800	
1400–1600	
1200–1400	
1000–1200	
800–1000	
600–800	
400–600	
200–400	
0–200	

Contour lines are drawn at 25m intervals and highlighted at 100m intervals.

SCALE: 1:50,000

0 kilometres 0.5   1
0 miles   0.5

GPX files for all routes can be downloaded free at www.cicerone.co.uk/996/GPX.

Mountain safety

Every mountain walk has its dangers, and those described in this guidebook are no exception. All who walk or climb in the mountains should recognise this and take responsibility for themselves and their companions along the way. The author and publisher have made every effort to ensure that the information contained in this guide was correct when it went to press, but, except for any liability that cannot be excluded by law, they cannot accept responsibility for any loss, injury or inconvenience sustained by any person using this book.

International distress signal *(emergency only)*
Six blasts on a whistle (and flashes with a torch after dark) spaced evenly for one minute, followed by a minute's pause. Repeat until an answer is received. The response is three signals per minute followed by a minute's pause.

Helicopter rescue
The following signals are used to communicate with a helicopter:

Help needed: raise both arms above head to form a 'Y'

Help not needed: raise one arm above head, extend other arm downward

Emergency telephone numbers
Mountain rescue: tel 140
European emergency number: tel 112
Fire: tel 122
Police: tel 133
Ambulance: tel 144

Weather reports
Alpine Association Weather: www.alpenverein.at/portal/wetter
Weather Austria: www.bergfex.com/oesterreich/wetter

Mountain rescue can be very expensive – be adequately insured.

Dachstein peaks and Gosau Glacier reflected in Gosaulacke (Walk 28)

Ferry on Grundlsee, departing from Gößl (Walk 21)

INTRODUCTION

On my first visit to Salzkammergut I hiked up through the Echerntal, the forest a patchwork of dark greens and reddish browns, flecked with the pale gold of larches. Mist clung to the sides of the valley, and waterfalls threaded their way silently down dark grey rock faces as I crunched up through October snow onto the edge of the Dachstein plateau. The following morning I woke early to watch the massive northeast face of the Niederer Oschsenkogel turn blood red in the first rays of the early morning sun; and later that day, followed a snowbound trail up towards Simonyhütte on the edge of the Hallstätter Glacier, watched by a group of ptarmigan which blended almost completely into the soft white slopes below Wildkarkogel. I have been returning to this breathtakingly beautiful part of Austria ever since.

Austria's Salzkammergut region is a wonderfully alluring sweep of landscape east of Salzburg, studded with lakes (there are some 76 of them in all) and bristling with mountain peaks, its sprawling karst plateaus and fractured glaciers rising above great glacier-scoured valleys and lush, forest-cloaked hillsides.

It's a fantastic area for walking, with an enormous range of trails, from easy lakeside strolls to challenging mountain walks and everything in

SALZKAMMERGUT AT A GLANCE

Austrian states: Salzburgerland, Upper Austria, Styria
Language: German
Religion: Predominantly Roman Catholic
Time zone: CET (GMT +1)
Currency: Euro
International dialling code: +43
Electricity: 240V/50Hz (standard European two-pin plug)

between, and the routes in this guide have been selected to cover something of this variety. All the routes in this book lie within the capabilities of the reasonably fit walker, without requiring any technical climbing or equipment. All of them are ludicrously easy to get to, with many lying less than an hour from Salzburg, and all of them accessible by public transport. Ferry routes crisscross the larger lakes, and there's a mountain railway on one peak. Each can be walked in a day, from a guesthouse in one of the many small lakeside towns and villages, or from a mountain hut – and there's plenty of scope to link some together to form longer through walks. In between hikes, there are seemingly limitless opportunities for a swim, ice caves and historic salt mines to visit, and wonderful Austrian food and hospitality to enjoy.

The area's history stretches back through several thousand years of highly organised salt mining, which developed into the extraordinarily rich Iron Age culture of the Hallstatt Period. Many centuries later, Salzkammergut was the summer residence of Emperor Franz Josef I, from where affairs of state of the vast Austro-Hungarian realms were administered. The whole Dachstein massif and Hallstatt area form a UNESCO World Heritage Site, and the Totes Gebirge forms part of the Northern Kalkalpen IBA. Hallstatt itself is hugely popular, but travel only a short distance and you can find quiet, uncluttered trails, hillsides studded with wildflowers, views which you will stay with you forever.

Writing this guide has been a hugely rewarding experience, the most challenging part of which was having to decide which walks not to include, since there are simply so many to choose from – and over a succession of trips to this part of Austria, has taken me along some of the most compellingly beautiful hiking trails I know.

GEOGRAPHY AND GEOLOGY

The Salzkammergut region lies east of Salzburg and straddles the borders of three Austrian states: Salzburgerland,

Upper Austria (Oberösterreich) and Styria (Steiermark). Unlike these Federal States (Länder or Bundesländer) the borders of Salzkammergut are a little imprecise, but essentially it stretches from Ebenau in the west to the River Steyr in the east, including the huge sprawl of the Totes Gebirge in the east and the Dachstein plateau in the south, and ending just beyond Scörfling and Gmunden in the north, where the hills abruptly melt away into the plains. What really ties it all together as a geographical area, however, is its long history of salt mining (the name Salzkammergut is derived from the words *salz* meaning salt, and *kammergut* which is an old term for a demesne, the lands belonging to a lord or king under the feudal system of land ownership) – but more on that later.

In any case, the mountains of the Salzkammergut region form part of the Northern Limestone Alps, or more specifically according to the Alpine Club's Classification of the Eastern Alps (AVE), comprise the following mountain groups: the Salzkammergut Mountains, the Upper Austrian Prealps, the Totes Gebirge and the Dachstein Mountains. Sweeping through them from south to north is the Traun, the area's main river.

Within this area, Salzkammergut contains an extraordinary number of lakes – some 76 of them, ranging in size from over 45km² (Attersee, the largest lake in Salzkammergut) to tiny alpine tarns, and in depth from 191m (Traunsee, the deepest lake in Austria) to just a few metres. The altitude of the larger lakes is generally between 500m and 700m. It is these lakes – *See* in German – in combination with

The trail to Loser crosses steep slopes above Loserhütte Altaussee (Walk 17)

the region's spectacular mountains, which perhaps more than anything else give Salzkammergut its special character.

The walks in this guide are centred around several of these lakes – Fuschlsee (Walks 1–3), Wolfgangsee (Walks 4–7), Mondsee (Walk 8), Traunsee (Walks 9–13), Altausseer See (Walks 16–19), Grundlsee (Walks 20–22), Hallstätter See (Walks 23–24) and Gossausee (Walks 28–30) – and visit a dozen or so more of them from these bases. The few walks that aren't centred on a lake are centred on the Dachstein (Walks 25–27), or around Bad Ischl (Walks 14–15).

The Dachstein and Totes Gebirge are huge karst plateaus, the former measuring around 20km by 30km and falling in an almost sheer wall on its southern edge. The Hohe Dachstein (2996m), located on this southern edge of the plateau, is the highest peak in the region, indeed the highest in either Upper Austria or Styria, with a topographic prominence of eighth highest in the Alps. The Dachstein plateau has numerous peaks over 2500m; however, most peaks in the Salzkammergut region are in the range of 1700m to 2200m, with those of the Totes Gebirge tending towards the higher end of this.

The salt deposits, from which the region has drawn so much of its wealth for over two millennia, were formed by the evaporation of seawater in the Hallstatt-Meliata Ocean, one of a number of smaller seas on

*Fossilised sea snails (*Trochactaeon*) beside Vorderer Gosausee (Walk 28)*

the margins of the Tethys Ocean during the Permian period, over 250 million years ago. These evaporites were later submerged once more, and overlaid with a thick layer of limestone formed from shells and other marine life deposited on the seabed around thriving reefs during the Triassic period, when the calcareous deposits and associated reefs forming the Dachstein massif developed to a thickness of over 1000m. Finally, after the closing of the ocean in the Jurassic period, the evaporite reserves were compressed into a diapir (a domed rock formation formed through a geological intrusion) which forced its way upwards into the overlying limestone. This limestone was subsequently displaced and shifted northwards to its present location as a system of nappes or overthrusts (known as the Juvavic and Tyrolic nappe systems, and to a lesser extent the Bajuvaric), forming the Dachstein, Totes Gebirge and Salzkammergut mountains.

The limestone of the Dachstein massif is extremely rich in marine fossils, such as Trochactaeon (an extinct sea snail) as well as corals, and the reddish limestone around Hallstatt constitutes one of the richest areas for ammonites anywhere in the world, with more than 500 ammonite species having been identified there. In contrast, the limestone of the Totes Gebirge around Altausseer See has fewer or no fossils.

The Dachstein, Totes Gebirge and Höllengebirge have a wealth of karst features such as rillenkarren, heel-print karren and karren pipes, and are pockmarked with dolines (hollows or basins in karst regions, typically funnel-shaped). They are also home to some spectacular caves, several of which can be visited – the Rieseneishöhle (Giant Ice Cave) and Mammuthhöhle (Mammut Cave) at Schönbergalm, and the Koppenbrüllerhöhle (Koppenbrüller Cave) between Obertraun and Bad Aussee. Slightly to the southwest of Salzkammergut on the edge of the Tennengebirge, and easily visited from Salzburg or on a return loop through Salzkammergut, the Eisriesenwelt is the largest ice cave in the world. Among the most impressive karst springs in Salzkammergut are the Strummern near Bad Mitterndorf, which gush up in springtime and early summer fed by snowmelt.

The Dachstein massif is the only part of the Salzkammergut region where glaciers still remain (the northernmost and easternmost not only in Austria but in the whole of the Alps), descending on the northern side of the Hohe Dachstein – the Hallstätter Glacier to the north (the largest of the group), the Gosau and Schneeloch glaciers to the west, and the Schladming

Hiking across the karst landscape below Simonyhütte, on the Dachstein Nature Trail (Walk 25)

On the trail from the Echerntal to Wiesberghaus after October snowfall (Walk 24)

Glacier to the east. Like elsewhere in the world and in the Austrian Alps in particular, they are shrinking rapidly, and their extent relative to even a few years ago is a sobering reminder of the ongoing effects of climate change and global warming. The Hallstätter Glacier has shrunk to half its size since 1850 (when it stretched beyond Unterer Eissee), retreating by an average of about 10m per year over the past decade, and in one year alone between 2008 and 2009 the height of its surface dropped by over 1m. Some say its volume may reduce by half – or even that it will be gone entirely – in just 30 years' time.

CLIMATE

Salzkammergut experiences a fairly typical Alpine climate of warm summers and snow-bound winters. However, there is a fair amount of variation across the region, between the lakes in the north such as Mondsee with their lower and more open surroundings, and the high karst plateaus of Dachstein and the Totes Gebirge further to the southeast – or even between one lake and another.

The hiking season in Salzkammergut begins in mid-May, which is also when most huts open for the summer, although particularly in higher areas you can expect to still encounter snow at this time, which will linger through to July, and there will be patches of snow in dolines right through the summer. June and July generally bring plenty of warm, sunny weather for hiking, with July usually having the highest temperatures of the year. August can be beautifully sunny, but also stormy, particularly in the afternoons – in which case, aim to finish your hike by midday or early afternoon. September generally brings more settled weather again, and the first snow usually arrives around the middle of October, by which time most mountain huts have closed.

The tables give recent average, maximum and minumum monthly temperatures (°C) for the months of April to November, for Bad Ischl and Feuerkogel.

Temperatures at Mondsee were found to be similar to those for Bad Ischl, if around a degree warmer; those at higher altitudes such as on Dachstein, slightly cooler than on Feuerkogel. Rainfall is highest in the summer months, with averages of around 175mm in Bad Ischl in July, slightly more in Hallstatt for the same month and over 200mm on Feuerkogel. Snowfall on the Höllengebirge reaches a depth of around 2.5m in January and February, more on Dachstein. January is generally the coldest month, with average valley temperatures of around -3°C, though possibly as low as -10°C, and at higher elevations dropping below this considerably.

Water temperatures in Salzkammergut's lakes rise into the low to mid-twenties Celsius during the summer months, with an average summer high of 26°C in Mondsee, 23°C in Halstätter See and 19°C in Grundlsee. Many of the lakes have

Bad Ischl (507m)

	Apr	May	Jun	Jul	Aug	Sept	Oct	Nov
Average monthly temperature (°C)	10.3	13.4	19.2	19	19.3	13.4	10.5	4.7
Absolute maximum temperature (°C)	28.7	30.9	36.4	35	35.7	28.8	25	21.6
Absolute minimum temperature (°C)	-3.4	0.4	6.3	7.1	6.2	1.3	0.2	-4.3

Feuerkogel (1618m)

	Apr	May	Jun	Jul	Aug	Sept	Oct	Nov
Average monthly temperature (°C)	3.9	7.1	12.9	13.2	14.1	8.6	7.1	2.2
Absolute maximum temperature (°C)	18.2	21.3	26.8	24.9	26.3	20.8	21.1	18.5
Absolute minimum temperature (°C)	-9.2	-6.1	1.8	4.2	1.4	-2.5	-5.1	-9.0

beaches, making an after-hike swim a particularly attractive option.

On balance, the best months for hiking in Salzkammergut are June, July and September, although the author has also enjoyed beautiful days of hiking in October, with a fresh 0.5m of snow on the Dachstein plateau.

Weather forecasts
Alpine Association Weather – www. alpenverein.at/portal/wetter/
Weather Austria – www.bergfex.com/ oesterreich/wetter/

WILDLIFE AND PLANTS

There's plenty of wildlife to look out for in Salzkammergut, and while it might not quite have the status of a birdwatching hotspot to the same degree as Neusiedler See, Kalkalpen or Hoher Tauern national parks, it is still incredibly rich in wildlife and plants.

Mammals to be seen include chamois (*Rupicapra rupicapra*), red deer (*Cervus elaphus*), roe deer (*Capreolus capreolus*), Alpine ibex (*Capra ibex*), marmot (*Marmota marmota*), red squirrel (*Sciurus vulgaris*, almost always with black fur when I've seen them), Alpine hare (*Lepus timidus*) and wild boar (*Sus scofa*). In the 1990s an attempt was made to reintroduce the brown bear into Austria's Northern Limestone Alps, to complement a lone male which had

Clockwise from top left: Mountain avens (Dryas octopetala); Alpine salamander (Salamandra atra); Gentian (Gentianella germanica); Alpine chough (Pyrrhocorax graculus)

inhabited the area since the 1970s; however, the last of their descendants disappeared in 2011, and the population is now considered extinct. Bat species include the greater mouse-eared (*Myotis myotis*), lesser horseshoe (*Rhinolophus hipposideros*), and the near-threatened Bechstein's bat (*Myotis bechsteinii*) and Barbastelle (*Barbastella barbastellus*).

The Alpine salamander (*Salamandra atra*), the range of which is limited to the Eastern and Central Alps as well as the Dinaric Alps in southeast Europe, and which is easily distinguished from the fire salamander by its all-black colouring, can be found in areas of Salzkammergut above 700m. Lakes and ponds provide a habitat for yellow-bellied toad (*Bombina variegata*) and other amphibians, while reptiles include the common adder (*Vipera berus*) and the non-venomous Aesculapian snake (*Zamenis longissimus*).

Alpine chough (*Pyrrhocorax graculus*) are commonly seen around mountain peaks, and there are several birds of prey to be on the lookout for, among them the majestic golden eagle (*Aquila chrysaetos*), goshawk (*Accipiter gentilis*), sparrow hawk (*Accipiter nisus*) and peregrine falcon (*Falco peregrinus*).

Other species of bird include Tengmalm's owl (*Aegolius funereus*), Eurasian eagle owl (*Bubo bubo*, unmistakable with its long tufted ears and huge size), wallcreeper (*Tichodroma muraria*), crag martin (*Ptyonoprogne*

rupestris), Alpine accentor (*Prunella collaris*), ptarmigan (*Lagopus muta*), hazel grouse (*Bonasa bonasia*), an Alpine subspecies of rock partridge (*Alectoris graeca saxatilis*), and several species of woodpecker including the grey-headed (*Picus canus*), black (*Dryocopus martius*), great spotted (*Dendrocopos major*), three-toed (*Picoides tridactylus*) and Eurasian green (*Picus viridis*). Your best chances of seeing the less common of these species are on some of the less frequented trails on the Totes Gebirge and Dachstein.

Great crested grebe (*Podiceps cristatus*), cormorant (*Phalacrocorax carbo*), grey heron (*Ardea cinerea*), tufted duck (*Aythya fuligula*) and plenty of other wading birds and waterfowl can be seen around the lakes.

Despite vast areas of forest having been cut down over the centuries to be used by the local salt works, especially around Ebensee, parts of Salzkammergut remain heavily forested. Deciduous and mixed forest give way to conifers at higher altitudes, in particular spruce (*Picea abies*), with larch (*Larix decidua*) adding a beautiful yellow-gold colour to the landscape in autumn, and dwarf mountain pine (*Pinus mugo*) clinging to the rocky limestone plateaus.

Wildflowers on Dachstein and the Totes Gebirge in particular are wonderful, with rhododendron (both *Rhododendron hirsutum* or hairy alpenrose, and *Rhodothamnus chamaecistus*), mountain avens (*Dryas octopetala*), Alpine toadflax (*Linaria alpina*), Edelweiß (*Leontopodium alpinum*), bellflower (*Canmpanula pulla*), and the large blue trumpet-shaped flowers of Clusius' gentian (*Gentiana clusii*).

HISTORY

The history of Salzkammergut begins some 7000 years ago, with the Neolithic mining of salt at Hallstatt, and extends through the extraordinary cultural richness of the Celtic Hallstatt Culture in the Early Iron Age, and the vast power and wealth of the Habsburg Empire and Austria-Hungary.

Neolithic, Celtic and Roman periods

Human habitation in what is now Austria dates back to the Middle Paleolithic Era, some 250,000 years ago, and archaeological finds show that Alpine valleys in the Salzkammergut region were already settled in the Neolithic period, at least 5000BC. From 3800BC to 2800BC the shores of Mondsee, Attersee and Traunsee in Salzkammergut were settled by Neolithic farmers now called the Mondsee Group, known for their stilt houses and copper artefacts. In 2011 the remains of these settlements at Mondsee and Attersee were inscribed on the UNESCO List of World Heritage Sites, along with other prehistoric pile dwellings around the Alps.

The earliest physical evidence of organised mining at Hallstatt dates

back to around 1500BC during the Bronze Age, although salt mining in the region is believed to stretch back much further – a Neolithic adze made from deer antler, found in 1838 at Hallstatt, is believed to have been used for salt mining as early as 5000BC. A wooden staircase discovered in the salt mines at Hallstatt in 2002 has been dated to 1344 or 1343BC, and during the period 800–450BC, associated with the Early Iron Age Hallstatt Culture, there is evidence of mining to a depth of 200m at Hallstatt. Around 450BC the spread of the Celtic La Tène Culture gradually superseded the Hallstatt Culture.

Around 400BC, a loose federation of Celtic tribes founded the Kingdom of Noricum, covering most of what are now Austria and Slovenia. The Romans arrived in what is now Austria around 200BC, and around 15BC they took the Celtic fortified settlement of Vedunia, renaming it Vindobona – better known today as Vienna. In 40AD Celtic Noricum was incorporated into the Roman Province of Noricum (the famous iron ore deposits of Noricum continued to be exploited, and produced the highly prized Noric steel used for Roman weaponry), and in 45AD Roman Juvavum (modern Salzburg) was declared a *municipium*.

Medieval Salzkammergut

Bavarian tribes began settling in the area east of Salzburg in the 6th century, and around 696 St Rupert, from the town of Regensburg in Bavaria, arrived in Salzburg at the invitation of Theodo of Bavaria, laying the foundations for the re-establishment of the Salzburg diocese. The great abbey at Mondsee was founded in 748, and in 798 the Roman Catholic Archdiocese of Salzburg was founded by St Boniface (an Anglo-Saxon missionary from Devon in England), as an ecclesiastical principality and state of the Holy Roman Empire.

In 976 the Duchy of Bavaria established an Eastern March or Ostmark as an eastern outpost, giving rise to the German word *Ostarrichi* meaning 'Eastern Realm', whence Austria. This Ostmark, which was then ruled by the Badenberg dynasty from Vienna, was made a duchy in 1156. Following the death of the last Badenberg the Ostmark was seized by Ottokar II of Bohemia; however, he was defeated in 1278 at the Battle of the Marchfeld, one of the largest battles of the Middle Ages, by Rudolf I of Germany, who then founded the Habsburg Empire.

Salzkammergut under the Habsburgs
Salt mining at Hallstatt and Altausee (the latter first recorded in 1147) thrived during the Middle Ages, supplying the Prince-Archbishopric of Salzburg and later the Habsburgs with this extremely valuable 'white gold', and giving the Salzkammergut region its name (from the words *salz* meaning salt, and *kammergut* which is an old term for a demesne, the lands belonging to a lord or king under the feudal system of land ownership). In 1311 Hallstatt was granted a market charter by Elisabeth, Queen of Germany, which specifically refers to salt production, and 1511 saw the construction of the Steeger Klause, a dam allowing the water level of Hallstätter See to be controlled in order to allow salt barges to sail down the River Traun. In 1595 construction began on a pipeline to carry brine from the mines at Hallstatt to Ebensee, where it was transformed into salt. The pipeline – completed in 1607, and last replaced after World War 2 – is still in use today, and is the oldest such pipeline in the world.

In 1823 Dr Josef Götz opened his first bathing salon in Bad Ischl, and a few years later in 1831 Archduke Franz Karl and Archduchess Sophie brought their infant son, the future Emperor Franz Josef, to Bad Ischl to celebrate his first birthday (the date, 18 August, is still celebrated in Bad Ischl). This kicked off a wave of popularity for the small town as a fashionable spa resort. From 1854 Emperor Franz Joseph and Queen Sisi took up residence at the Kaiservilla in Bad Ischl, which was to become their summer residence for the next 81 years. During this period, a paddle steamer was launched for the first time on Wolfgangsee in 1873, work began on a narrow-gauge railway between Salzburg and Bad Ischl (the Salzkammergut-Lokalbahn) in 1890, and the Schafbergbahn mountain railway was opened in 1893. When on 28 July 1914, following the assassination of Archduke Franz Ferdinand of Austria (heir presumptive to the throne of Austria-Hungary) and his wife in Sarajevo, Emperor Franz Joseph signed a declaration of war on Serbia – thus precipitating Europe into World War 1 – he did so while at his summer residence in Bad Ischl.

It was also during the 19th century that geological exploration of the Dachsein massif began in earnest, a process associated in particular with one man, the great Austrian geographer and Alpine explorer Friedrich Simony. Simony began his pioneering research of the Dachstein in 1840. In 1843 he was the first to spend a night on the summit of the Hoher Dachstein, and in 1847 he made the first winter ascent of the Hoher Dachstein. Simony's book

SALT MINING IN SALZKAMMERGUT – A BRIEF TIMELINE

5000BC – A Neolithic adze made from deer antler, found in 1838 at Hallstatt, is believed to be from this period and to have been used for salt mining.

1500BC – Earliest physical evidence of organised mining at Hallstatt.

800–450BC – Early Iron Age Hallstatt Culture. Evidence of mining to a depth of 200m.

c350BC – Mining at Hallstatt comes to an abrupt end following a massive landslide, which buries most of the high valley, and mining begins in a different location nearby.

1147 – First mention of salt mining in Altaussee.

1284 – Construction of the Rudolfsturm (Rudolf's Tower) at the salt mines in Hallstatt, both as a defensive tower and as the residence of the mining operations manager.

1311 – Hallstatt granted a market charter by Elisabeth, Queen of Germany.

1511 – Construction of the Steeger Klause, a dam allowing the water level of Hallstätter See to be controlled in order to allow salt barges to sail down the River Traun.

1595–1607 – Construction of pipeline carrying brine from the mines at Hallstatt to Ebensee, where it is transformed into salt.

1750 – The timber buildings of Hallstatt's old town are destroyed by fire, following which it is rebuilt in Baroque style.

1846 – Johann Ramsauer, a mine official at Hallstatt, begins a systematic investigation of the Hallstatt burial grounds. His discoveries lead to the period of the Iron Age c800–450BC becoming known as the 'Hallstatt Period'.

1997 – Dachstein-Hallstatt Cultural landscape inscribed on the UNESCO List of World Heritage Sites.

Rudolfsturm, at the entrance to Hallstatt salt mine

Die Seen des Salzkammergutes was published in 1850.

Modern history

The First Republic of Austria (Republik Österreich) was created in 1920, following the end of the Habsburg Empire in 1918. Austria became part of Hitler's Germany when the Nazis invaded in 1938, and in a twist of history Hitler ordered his priceless collection of looted art treasures, bound for his proposed new museum in Linz, to be hidden in the salt mine at Bad Aussee in 1943. He later gave instructions that they should all be destroyed in the event of a German defeat; however, local mine workers removed the explosives left for this purpose and hid them in the woods, thus saving well-known masterpieces such as the Ghent Altarpiece and works by Rembrandt and Michelangelo.

Modern Austria was established as an independent, neutral state in 1955 by the Austrian State Treaty (Staatsvertrag), and joined the EU in 1995. In 1997 the Dachstein-Hallstatt Cultural Landscape was inscribed on the UNESCO List of World Heritage Sites.

GETTING TO AUSTRIA

Salzburg, the main gateway to Salzkammergut, can be reached easily enough by plane or, better still, by rail. The other useful gateway city, Linz, no longer has direct flights from the UK, but can still be reached by train.

By air

Easyjet, Ryanair and British Airways all fly direct to Salzburg from the UK; Eurowings operates direct routes to Salzburg from several cities in Germany, and Finnair flies direct from Helsinki. At the time of writing, direct flights from the UK to Linz had been withdrawn, but Easyjet, Austrian Airlines, British Airways, Eurowings and Ryanair all fly direct from the UK to Vienna. There are direct flights to Vienna from plenty of other European cities including Amsterdam, Brussels, Paris, Madrid, Oslo and Stockholm, as well as from the United States and Canada. Flights from the United States and Canada to Salzburg involve a stop in Vienna, Frankfurt or elsewhere.

By rail

Getting to Austria by rail from the UK is a far more straightforward proposal than many people realise. It's also possible to get there for a similar fare to a flight, providing you book well in advance (see below), and once you factor in the extra cost of a checked-in rucksack to an airfare, rail travel is not necessarily more expensive than flying, contrary to popular opinion. In addition, a journey by rail from London to Salzburg also emits roughly one eighth of the carbon dioxide produced by a flight over the same route.

For a trip to Salzkammergut, the two best rail routes from the UK are London to Salzburg, and London to Linz. The fastest of these is London to Salzburg – meaning, London to

Brussels via Eurostar, Brussels to Frankfurt on a high speed ICE, Frankfurt to either Stuttgart or Munich, and from there to Salzburg – a journey which can take under 11 hours, city centre to city centre. London to Linz works quite well on an overnight sleeper, arriving in Linz early in the morning.

The best way to book is through Deutsche Bahn (www.bahn.com); online bookings can be made three months in advance; however, phone bookings can be made six months in advance through the Deutsche Bahn UK call centre (tel 020 8339 4708), and ideally you should aim at using the latter to get the lowest possible fares (Super Sparpreis). The route taken for the lower fares tends to be via Brussels. Deutsche Bahn also make it possible to add a stopover (for no extra charge), even when booking online – Stuttgart or Cologne, for example, are well placed for breaking the journey between Salzburg and London into two.

Travelling to Salzburg by rail from elsewhere in Europe, you can expect a journey time of around 8.5 hours from Brussels, 7.5 hours from Paris, 6 hours from Berlin and 5.5 hours from Zürich, to give just a few examples. From Vienna, it's just over 1 hour by rail to Linz and 2.5 hours to Salzburg.

It's also worth remembering that Eurostar, TGV, Deutsche Bahn, OEBB and Thalys all adhere to a mutual guarantee, meaning that if any one service of these operators is cancelled/delayed and this causes you to miss your connecting service run by one of the others, your ticket will be changed to the next departure at no charge, a very simple and straightforward process.

One caveat is the section of the journey between Cologne and Brussels, or vice versa. The otherwise wonderfully slick and efficient German trains sometimes have problems with the switch to Belgian overhead power cables. When travelling back to the UK on this route it's best to allow at least an extra hour over and above the recommended arrival time for a connecting Eurostar from Brussels. That way, if there is any delay or problem with a train arriving from Cologne, you'll have enough time to take a local Belgian train from

Aachen to Brussels (slower, and with a change at Welkenraedt, but it will get there on time and unlike the next German ICE train, it won't be utterly packed).

The best source of information on rail travel in Europe is the excellent www.seat61.com.

For more information on Salzburg and Linz, see Appendix B.

GETTING AROUND BY PUBLIC TRANSPORT

Public transport in Austria is excellent, and it's extremely easy to get to and around Salzkammergut by local bus or train, from Salzburg, Linz or other cities.

Trisselwand summit cross (Walk 18)

To summarise, the main approaches to Salzkammergut and the hikes described in this guide, from Salzburg and Linz, are as follows:

- Salzburg–Fuschl am See–St Gilgen–Strobl–Bad Ischl (bus)
- Attnang-Puchheim (a rail junction, from where there are trains to both Salzburg and Linz)–Gmunden–Ebensee–Bad Ischl–Bad Goisern–Hallstatt–Obertraun–Bad Aussee (rail)

These two routes, intersecting at Bad Ischl in the heart of Salzkammergut, make it very straightforward to travel around the area without a car. All the walks described in this guide can be reached by public transport (with the exception of two walks, which can be reached by a fixed-fare taxi service which costs little more than a local bus).

Bus

The main bus routes which you're likely to use getting to the routes in this guide, with their respective timetables, are:

- 140 Salzburg–Mondsee https://salzburg-verkehr.at
- 150 Salzburg–Fuschl am See–St Gilgen–Strobl–Bad Ischl Ischl https://salzburg-verkehr.at
- 156 St Gilgen–Mondsee https://salzburg-verkehr.at (connecting with bus no. 150)
- 542 Bad Ischl–Bad Goisern–Gosausee (connecting with bus no. 952) www.postbus.at/

- 543 Gosaumühle Hallstatt and Obertraun www.ooevv.at
- 546 Bad Ischl–Strobl–St Wolfgang www.ooevv.at
- 950 Stainach–Bad Mitterndorf–Bad Aussee www.verbundlinie.at
- 952 Bad Ischl–Bad Aussee www.verbundlinie.at
- 955 Bad Aussee–Altaussee www.verbundlinie.at
- 956 Bad Aussee–Grundlsee www.verbundlinie.at

Further details of individual bus and train routes are given in the introduction to each section and route.

Train tickets should be bought from the ticket office or ticket machine at the railway station (smaller stations don't have a ticket office, in which case allow yourself enough time for a possible queue at the ticket machine). You can't buy a ticket on the train on these short, local routes, and if you travel without a ticket (and there will be a ticket inspector on most train journeys) you risk paying a fine. You can buy bus tickets from the driver when boarding the bus.

By far the busiest route into Salzkammergut is the 150 bus from Salzburg to Bad Ischl, and the train from there to Hallstatt (Hallstatt railway station is on the opposite side of the lake to the town itself, but a boat between them connects with train arrival times). The 150 often fills up completely in the summer (when this happens, a second bus generally arrives, though not always), so try to get to the bus stop early to be at the front of the queue (at Salzburg Hauptbahnhof, this is stop F; at Bad Ischl bus/train station, it's the second platform south of the railway station building). You can buy tickets online, but this won't guarantee you a seat if the bus is full.

It's also worth bearing in mind that while the 150 bus runs quite late in the evening (the last departure from Salzburg on weekdays is at 2315), some of the other bus services don't run this late, though all generally start from fairly early in the morning. Also, while the trains between Bad Ischl and Obertraun run every hour or so until about 2100 on weekdays, some services don't continue from Obertraun to Bad Aussee, and the last service departing from Bad Aussee for Obertraun and Bad Ischl is much earlier, around 1815.

If you finish your trip with the walks in the Gosautal (Walks 28–30) you can return to Salzburg by taking the 470 bus from Gosau to Golling, and the train from there into Salzburg; or if you do Walk 30 as a through hike, descend to Annaberg im Lammertal and take the 471 bus (less frequent) to Abtenau, changing onto the the 470 from there to Golling from where you can take the train to Salzburg.

Ferries

Ferries operate on several of the lakes in Salzkammergut, and provide a lovely way to get around. Some ferry routes are included as an integral part of a walk. The ferries which you are

Ferry between Hoisn (Walk 9) and Gmunden on Traunsee

likely to find useful for the walks in this guide are:

- Traunsee (return on Walk 9) www.traunseeschifffahrt.at
- Wolfgangsee (optional alternative to bus on Walks 4–7) www.schaf bergbahn.at
- Hallstätter See (to reach the start of Walk 24 from the railway station) www.hallstattschifffahrt.at
- Grundlsee (optional alternative to bus on Walks 20–22) www. schifffahrt-grundlsee.at
- Toplitzsee (integral part of Walk 20) www.schifffahrt-grundlsee.at

Fares are generally quite reasonable, for example €6 for Hoisn to Gmunden on Traunsee (Walk 9), €10 for the return trip across Toplitzsee (Walk 20).

Cable cars and mountain railways

There are cable car (*seilbahn*) routes on several mountains in Salzkammergut, and some have been used to get to the start of a route, with a hike back down included in some of the routes.

- Dachstein-Krippenstein Seilbahn (descent on Walk 24, ascent and/or descent on Walks 25–27 depending on whether you connect them with Walk 24, and base yourself at Gjaidalm or Wiesberghaus for a few nights as recommended) https://dachstein-salzkammergut.com/
- Feuerkogel Seilbahn (ascent and descent on Walks 11 and 12) www.feuerkogel.info

Feuerkogel cable car (Walks 11 and 12)

- Katrin Seilbahn (ascent on Walk 14) www.katrinseilbahn.com
- Zwölferhorn Seilbahn (ascent on Walk 5) www.zwoelferhorn.at

There are also cable cars at Gosausee and on Grünberg, which have not been included in the walks but could be used to shorten them if preferred:

- Grünberg Seilbahn (Walk 9) https://gruenberg.info/
- Gosaukamm Seilbahn (Walk 30) www.dachstein.at
- The Schafbergbahn mountain railway is included in the ascent of Scahfberg (Walk 7) www.schafbergbahn.at

ACCOMMODATION

Most of the walks in this guide are from towns and villages, where there are guesthouses (*Gasthof*) and pensions (*Pension*), with the exception of Walks 25–27 which are from huts on the Dachstein plateau (while they could also be done as day trips from Obertraun or Hallstatt this is not recommended). Bed and breakfast at a small gasthof in Salzkammergut is likely to set you back at least €35–€50 per person, more in Hallstatt and Bad Ischl. Recommendations for places to stay in Salzburg are in Appendix B.

For the nights spent in mountain huts (*Hütte*) for Walks 25–27 (or for other walks you might decide to extend, such as Walk 24) there will usually be a choice of shared rooms with bunks (*Mehrbettzimmer*),

Hallstatt viewed across Hallstätter See from the ferry

a shared dorm with mattresses (*Matratzenlager*), and in larger huts double/twin rooms (*Zweibettzimmer*). You need to bring your own sheet sleeping bag liner (*Hüttenschlafsack*) for overnights in huts (blankets or quilts are provided, so a sleeping bag is not required) and a towel. Expect to pay around €30 for an overnight stay in a mountain hut (shared room). Breakfast is not usually included in the room price, and usually costs around €12 extra; half board (including three-course dinner, breakfast and 1l of tea) costs around €33. Austrian Alpine Club (Österreichischer Alpenverein or OAV in German) members get a discount in huts (members: *Mitglieder*, non-members: *Nicht-Mitglieder*).

For more information on mountain huts go to the Alpenverein website www.alpenverein.at and click

on Hütte, then under Gebirgsgruppe choose Salzkammergut-berge or Dachsteingebierge.

FOOD

Früstuck (breakfast) in a pension is likely to consist of a selection of hams and cheeses, bread, butter and jam, eggs cooked to order, and a pot of coffee or tea; larger hotels have more extensive buffet breakfasts. Freshwater fish features prominently on menus, in particular char (*Saibling*), pike-perch (*Zander*) and trout (*Forelle*), alongside traditional dishes such as roast pork with dumplings. Vegetarian options are sometimes overly loaded with cheese, but *Spinatknödel* (spinach dumplings) and *Kasnudeln* (a kind of giant ravioli) are generally both delicious. Dishes made with

31

MENU READER

Apfelstrudel: apple strudel
Bärlauchcremesuppe: wild garlic soup
Bratwurst: sausages, usually served with sauerkraut
Frittatensuppe: beef broth with strips of pancake
Tiroler Gröstl: fried potatoes and egg with pancetta and masses of fried onions, usually served in a frying pan
Gulaschsuppe: rich, slightly spicy goulash soup
Kaiserschmarrn: chopped, fluffy pancakes sprinkled with butter and sugar, caramelised under the grill, and served with fruit compote
Kartoffelsalat: potato salad
Kasnudeln: large, usually potato- and cheese-filled ravioli, topped with melted butter
Käsespätzle: cheese noodles served in a pan and garnished with fried onions
Käspressknödelsuppe: beef broth with cheese dumpling
Knödel: dumpling
Palatschinken: pancakes
Rindsuppe: beef soup
Saibling auf Müllerin-Art: fried char with potatoes, butter and lemon
Suppe: soup
Schweinsbraten: roast pork, traditionally served with dumplings
Vegetarisch: vegetarian
Wiener Schnitzel: pan-fried, breaded veal cutlet

Kaiserschmarrn at Simonyhütte (Walk 25)

seasonal ingredients such as wild garlic (*Bärlauch*) and porcini mushrooms (*Steinpilz*) are always worth looking out for. You'll find at least one bakery (*Bäckerei*) in even small towns, where you can buy sandwiches and pastries, or bread for a picnic.

For more food vocabulary, see Appendix D.

LANGUAGE

The official language in Austria is German, which is the language taught at schools and used in spoken and written media. However, the Bavarian dialect (also referred to as Austro-Bavarian), or *Bairisch*, is spoken widely (but not written), and there are several words and phrases in widespread use which you'll encounter in Salzkammergut, which you won't find in standard German. For example, the typical Austrian greetings *Grüß Gott!* and *Servus!* (both meaning Hi!/ Hello!), or *Pfiat di!* (meaning Bye!), and the words for several types of food, for example *Erdäpfel* instead of *Kartoffeln* for potato.

English is widely spoken in Salzkammergut, and where it is not, there will generally be someone on hand (the gasthof owner's son or daughter, for example) who does speak some English. As when travelling anywhere else in the world, making the effort to learn a few basic words and phrases will usually be greatly appreciated.

See Appendix D for a list of basic words and phrases.

Hoher Dachstein and Niederer Dachstein and the Hallstätter glacier (Walks 24 and 25)

MONEY

Most towns of even a moderate size in Salzkammergut have ATMs, and you can pay for most things (accommodation, meals, shopping, train tickets, cable car journeys and so on) by credit or debit card. There are a few cases where you'll need cash (or cash would be preferred), such as for short ferry trips or a beer in a hut.

Some huts accept card payments, some don't (cards are accepted at Wiesberghaus and Gjaidalm, for example; Simonyhütte accepts debit cards, but not credit cards); most guesthouses and hotels accept card payments; however, for a small pension (and notably, Gasthof Gosausee) you should expect to pay in cash.

A few examples of costs are given below:

- B&B in small/mid-range guesthouse €35–€45
- Overnight stay in a mountain hut €30 (shared room) – €40 (double room)
- Breakfast in a mountain hut €12
- Half board in a mountain hut (excluding price of room) €33
- Main course of grilled zander in mid-priced restaurant €15
- Main course of Spinatknödel in mid-priced restaurant €9
- Main course of Wiener Schnitzel in mid-priced restaurant €10
- Bowl of soup €3.50
- Sandwich in bakery €4.50
- Cup of coffee €2.50
- Local beer (0.5l) €3.50

- Local bus ticket €2.50 (Bad Aussee to Altaussee), €11 (Salzburg to Bad Ischl)
- Local train ticket €4.50 (Bad Ischl to Ebensee), €7.40 (Bad Ischl to Bad Aussee)
- Ferry journey (Gmunden to Ebensee) €12
- Cable car journey (one way/ return) €18/€26 (Zwölferhorn) – €32/€32 (Dachstein, stations I–III)

PHONES

The international dialling code for Austria is +43; omit the initial 0 from a local area code when calling from an international phone. Mobile coverage is good in the mountains, although some walks in this guide are in areas with no mobile coverage (in which case, this is noted in the walk introduction). In general, huts can only be contacted by phone (not by sms) or email.

MAPS

For planning purposes, the best general area map covering the entire Salzkammergut region and Dachstein is the Salzkammergut Berge Seen Trail map (1:90,000), available free at tourist offices throughout the region. At 1:50,000 the two-sheet set from Kompass, Salzkammergut (229 sheets 1 and 2) is very useful.

Local tourist offices also have some detailed hiking maps of their

PUBLIC HOLIDAYS

The following dates are observed as public holidays in Austria, meaning that public transport will be restricted to a Sunday service at best, and shops will be closed. Those listed in italics are only observed in some states.

1 January	New Year's Day	(movable)	Whit Monday (the day after Pentecost)
6 January	Epiphany	(movable)	Corpus Christi (60 days after Easter)
19 March	*St Joseph's Day (Styria)*	15 August	Assumption of the Virgin Mary
(movable)	Good Friday	*24 September*	*St Rupert's Day (Salzburg)*
(movable)	Easter Monday	26 October	National Holiday (Declaration of Neutrality)
1 May	National Holiday	1 November	All Saints' Day
4 May	*St Florian's Day (Upper Austria)*	8 December	Immaculate Conception
30 May	Ascension Day	24–26 December	Christmas

areas, which are definitely worth picking up. These include:
- Fuschlseeregion (1:37,000) covering Walks 1–8
- Naturerlebniskarte Mondseeland (1:35,000) covering Walks 1–4, 7 and 8
- Ferienregion Traunsee (1:50,000) covering Walks 9–12
- Naturerlebniskarte Bad Ischl (1:45,000) covering Walks 14 and 15
- Naturerlebniskarte Ausseerland Salzkammergut (1:50,000) covering Walks 16–23

As far as more detailed maps go, the best ones to get are the AV (Alpenverein) 1:25,000 sheets – those covering some of the routes in this guide are as follows:
- 14 Dachstein
- 15/1 Totes Gebirge West
- 15/2 Totes Gebirge Mitte

WAYMARKING

As elsewhere in Austria, trails in Salzkammergut are well marked with a uniform red and white trail blazing, painted on rocks or tree trunks or similar. At least at trail junctions they are also indicated by signposts (usually yellow) which would typically include one or more of the following: timing, trail number and difficulty (the latter indicated by a blue, red

or black dot, corresponding to easy, medium and difficult).

HIKING WITH KIDS

Salzkammergut is a fantastic area for family hiking – easily accessible, with wonderful scenery and enough variety that it's unlikely to ever become boring for kids (or parents!). Beaches at many of the lakes mean there's ample opportunity for a post-hike swim, there are caves to visit and ferries to travel on (not to mention a mountain railway), there are birds, butterflies and Alpine salamanders to spot, wonderful mountain huts and guesthouses, and – very importantly – there is Kaiserschmarrn. All of the walks in this guidebook were done with my daughter when she was eight

or nine years old, making for some of the most rewarding hiking trips I have ever done.

LONGER ROUTES

Salzkammergut is very well set up for day hikes, giving you the luxury of hiking without a full pack. There are also, however, several excellent multi-day routes to tempt you. Launched in 2017, the Salzkammergut Berge Seen Trail is a 350km trek across the length and breadth of Salzkammergut, connecting 35 lakes, generally along very easy trails but with some tougher variants as well. The Dachstein Rundwanderweg is a 121km circuit of the Dachstein massif, which can be walked in around eight stages.

LOW IMPACT HIKING

Large numbers of visitors inevitably place a degree of strain on the environment, from trail erosion to waste management, so you should do all you can to minimise your impact.

- Carry all litter out with you after a hike (and don't leave it at huts).
- Don't buy plastic bottles of mineral water – carry a refillable flask and/or pouches. Tap water in Austria is fine to drink (and in the very few cases where it mightn't be, such as some of the taps outside a hut, there should be a sign to tell you so – 'kein trinkwasser' means it is not drinking water).
- Keep to established trails – walking on either side of a path simply widens it, destroying plant life and increasing erosion.
- Close gates behind you to prevent livestock wandering off.
- Use toilets at guesthouses and huts, not on the trail – it takes several months for toilet paper to fully decompose, and no one enjoys stumbling upon it during a hike.
- Use local public transport whenever possible, and where possible travel to Austria by rail rather than flying to reduce carbon emissions.

SAFETY AND EMERGENCIES

The routes in this guide follow well-kept trails that are clearly marked, requiring no special equipment or climbing skills, in an area which sees plenty of hikers and is very accessible. Nevertheless, like anywhere else in the mountains, sudden changes in weather or a simple sprain can turn what started out as an easy walk into something much more challenging, and anyone venturing into the mountains should be aware of potential dangers, be prepared to administer basic first aid and know how to react in an emergency.

- Leave a description of your planned routes with someone at home.
- Let someone at your accommodation, whether mountain hut or guesthouse, know your plans for the day.
- Check weather forecasts, and don't set off on high or exposed routes in bad or deteriorating weather.
- Always carry adequate warm and waterproof clothing.
- Always carry enough water and food.
- Always carry sufficient navigational aids – maps, smart phone, compass, GPS – and know how to use them.
- Always carry a basic first aid kit, a torch, an emergency bag or 'space blanket', and a whistle for attracting attention.
- In cold or extreme weather, be alert to any of the symptoms of exposure or hypothermia: loss of co-ordination, slurred speech, numbness in hands and feet,

shivering, shallow breathing or impaired vision. If hypothermia is suspected, get the victim out of the wind/rain, replace wet clothing with dry garments, keep the victim warm and give hot fluids and foods with high sugar and carbohydrate levels.

- Know the internationally recognised emergency signal: six audible or visible signs (whistle, torch etc) spaced evenly for one minute, followed by a minute's pause. (The answer is three signals per minute followed by a minute's pause.)

- Know the two signals for helicopter rescue: both arms raised above the head in a 'Y' shape means help needed; one arm raised above the head and one arm pointing downwards means help not needed.

- Make sure your travel insurance covers hiking (some policies don't). Membership of the Austrian Alpine Club (https://aacuk.org.uk/) also includes comprehensive insurance for mountain rescue services (worldwide, not just in Austria).

Mountain rescue

Austria has a well-established mountain rescue service (tel 140), which like similar services elsewhere in the world relies on the bravery of a few individuals. Never call for mountain rescue services in anything but a genuine emergency. If you do need to call mountain rescue services, be prepared to supply the following information:

- Your name and that of the person injured
- Type of accident, number of people involved, urgency
- Location of accident, including route/trail number and approximate altitude
- Weather conditions, including wind and visibility.

Note than mountain rescue services are not free in Austria, and costs for helicopter rescue, SAR or other services will need to be covered by the individual(s) requiring them, or their insurance policy (membership of the Austrian Alpine Club (https://aacuk.org.uk/) includes comprehensive insurance for mountain rescue services).

Emergency healthcare

EU citizens are covered in the event of needing emergency health treatment in Austria on production of a valid European Health Insurance Card (EHIC). With the UK's decision to leave the EU, the future of this arrangement for British citizens is uncertain, so check before you travel.

Emergency telephone numbers:
- Mountain rescue 140
- European emergency number 112
- Fire 122
- Police 133
- Ambulance 144

Ticks

Ticks are present in Austria – as they are throughout much of Europe – and

Mountain rescue helicopter picking up an injured climber after a fall on the Donnerkogel Klettersteig above Vorderer Gosausee

tick bites carry a risk of infection with European tick-borne encephalitis and Lyme disease. Before that sets off too many alarm bells, a tick bite does not necessarily mean that you have become infected – not all ticks carry the bacteria leading to Lyme disease or European tick-borne encephalitis, and not all tick bites lead to infection. However, both are highly unpleasant, debilitating, and in some cases fatal, diseases, and it's well worth knowing how to minimise your chances of contracting them.

The best form of protection against ticks is avoidance – wear long trousers and long-sleeved tops when walking through the undergrowth or long grass, or through the forest, along with a hat, particularly in late spring or early summer (when ticks are at their most common). Check your skin and scalp (and those of children if you're hiking with kids) when you finish your walk in the evening (a tick's body is brown and about the size of a pinhead).

In the event that you do find a tick attached to your skin, remove it as soon as possible – the risk of infection becomes higher if the tick remains undetected and is not removed within 24 hours. Ticks should be removed carefully using a special tick-removing tool such as the O'Tom Tick Twister (www.ticktwister.co.uk). Do not pull, squeeze or crush the tick's abdomen, or use irritants or cigarettes to encourage it to drop off you – doing so will cause it to regurgitate and

Fuschl am See from Ellmau (Walk 2)

therefore increase the risk of infection considerably. Instead, slip the head of the tick-tool under the tick's body, as close to your skin as possible, and twist gently. Once removed, clean the wound with alcohol or iodine, and make a note of the date you were bitten. A rash or fever a few days or more after the bite, or a red area spreading around the bite site, are signs that you may need further medical treatment. For more information about ticks and tick-borne diseases see the website of the British Mountaineering Council (www.thebmc.co.uk) and www.masta.org/tickalert/.

Water

Tap water in Austria is perfectly safe to drink, so there's no need to buy bottled water. If a source of water is unsafe (such as the separate water supply for the sinks in the toilets at a mountain hut, as opposed to the sinks in the bathroom) there would normally be a sign saying 'kein trinkwasser' (not drinking water). Springs are noted where they are found on a route and reliable. At some huts (eg Gjaidalm) there is a charge for tap water ordered by the glass with meals or at the bar. If in doubt, a Sawyer Mini Filter weighs less than 60g and takes up almost no space in your pack.

USING THIS GUIDE

The 30 walks in this guidebook are grouped by area – usually by lake – starting in the west and progressing east, then south. The arrangement of individual routes is not a reflection of their technical difficulty, length or duration. The information boxes at the start of each walk give a summary of essentials: start and finish point, total distance covered (in km), estimated walking time, ascent, descent and maximum altitude (in metres), and a brief description of the type(s) of terrain covered. They also include recommended maps, public transport, and en route refreshments options. The subsequent walk introduction provides a brief feel for the walk.

Walk grades

The walks in this guide have been graded as easy, medium of difficult:

Easy: implies a short (half day) walk on good, clear trails with little significant ascent or descent.

Medium: implies a longer walk (up to a full day) on good trails, with a greater amount of ascent and descent.

Difficult: implies a walk which is more challenging, on higher and possibly more remote terrain, with some short, mildly exposed sections secured with cables.

While subjective, it is hoped these grades will give the reader a quick idea of their level of difficulty relative to one another. The grades do not correlate to any other system of grading, or to the blue (easy), red (medium) and black (difficult) trail grades used on local signposts and walk descriptions. Although some of the 'difficult' walks include short, mildly exposed sections, most experienced walkers will still probably find them quite easy – none are via ferrata routes in the proper sense, and none require any climbing skills or equipment.

View across Traunsee from the waterfront at Ebensee

Autumn colours on Falkenstein pilgrimage trail (Walk 6)

Timings

The timing given in the box preceding the route description refers to an average walking speed, and does not include breaks or stopping time at summits or other points of interest.

Altitudes and distances

Altitudes and distances are given in metres and kilometres throughout.

Abbreviations

Within the route descriptions, north, south, east and west and intermediate compass bearings have been abbreviated N, S, E and W respectively. Left and right are abbreviated to L and R.

Spelling

Local (German) spelling has been used, for example Hallstätter See rather than Lake Hallstatt – with a few notable exceptions (Austria instead of Österreich, Upper Austria and Styria instead of Oberösterreich and Steiermark respectively).

Sketch maps

Routes are illustrated with maps at a scale of 1:50,000. Information on more detailed maps is given in the introduction to each walk.

Food and lodging

Recommendations for where to stay are given in the section introductions; information on refreshment stops on a route, including huts providing both food and accommodation is given within the route description itself.

GPX files

GPX files for each walk can be downloaded at www.cicerone.co.uk/996/GPX.

FUSCHLSEE, WOLFGANGSEE AND MONDSEE

Ferry on Wolfgangsee, below Schafberg (Walk 7)

Schafberg (Walk 7) viewed from St Lorenz, on Mondsee (Walk 8)

Fuschlsee lies 20km east of Salzburg at an altitude of 664m, and is generally the first of the Salzkammergut lakes encountered when approaching the region from Salzburg. The lake is around 4km long and just over 67m deep, and surrounded on the south by the long ridge of Filbling (1307m, Walk 3), and in its northeast corner by Schober (1328m) and Elmaustein (994m, Walk 2), which along with Almkogel (1030m, Walk 8) and the Drachenwand (1176m) divide Fuschlsee from nearby Mondsee, into which it drains by the Fuschler Ache. There's a beautiful walk around the lake (Walk 1). The best base on Fuschlsee for the walks in this guide is the small town of Fuschl am See, at the east end of the lake.

Less than 5km east of Fuschlsee, **Wolfgangsee** is around 10.5km long with a maximum depth of 114m. At its midway point, a protrusion in the southern shoreline pinches the lake into a narrow strait, just 200m wide, called Die Enge. The western half of the lake around St Gilgen is also known as Abersee. While the northern shore of Wolfgangsee is dominated by Schafberg (1782m, Walk 7), the southern shore is home to a number of peaks including (from west to east) Zwölferhorn (1522m, Walk 5), the Bleckwand (1516m), the prominent Sparber (1502m), and running from east to west behind these, the Osterhorngruppe. The border between the two states of Salzburgerland and Upper Austria runs across the slopes of Schafberg. The lake is named after St Wolfgang, bishop of Regensburg in Bavaria, who came to Wolfgangsee as a hermit towards the end of his life and built the first church here in the late 10th century (Finkelstein, Walk 6). The Pligrimage Church in the town of St Wolfgang itself has a well-known altarpiece by the 15th-century Tyrolean master, Michael Pacher. The town of St Gilgen at the east end of the lake is the most convenient base for the walks in this guide.

Mondsee is divided from its southern neighbours by Schafberg (which looks particularly impressive from this side), Almkogel (1130m, Walk 8) and the striking crags of the Drachenwand, the top of which can be reached by an excellent via ferrata route, while the hills above the lake's northern shore are much lower. The Neolithic Mondsee Group inhabited the Mondsee area around 3800–2800BC, living in stilt houses which form part of the UNESCO designated Prehistoric Pile Dwellings of the Alps, and making copper artefacts ('Ötzi the Iceman', the Copper Age man whose mummified remains were discovered in the Ötzal Alps, was found with an axe made from Mondsee copper). Mondsee Abbey, founded in the 8th century, is best known as one of the film locations for *The Sound of Music*. Mondsee is also home to a small museum dedicated to the old Salzkammergut-Lokalbahn railway (www.museum-mondsee. at). St Lorenz makes the best base for hiking in the area, right below the Drachenwand.

View of Mondsee from Almkogel (Walk 8)

TRANSPORT

Bus no. 150 stops at Fuschl am See (Walks 1–3), St Gilgen (Walks 4–7) and Strobl on its route between Salzburg and Bad Ischl. Bus no. 546 runs from Bad Ischl to Strobl to St Wolfgang (Walks 6–7). Bus no. 140 runs between St Gilgen and Mondsee, stopping at St Lorenz (Walk 8). Other bus services: during the summer there's a twice-weekly minibus from Strobl to Postalm (Mondays and Fridays), and from St Wolfgang to Schwarzensee (Mondays and Fridays).

Ferries run between St Gilgen and Strobl, calling at Fürberg, Ried, St Wolfgang and Gschwendt (www. schafbergbahn.at).

The historic Schafbergbahn mountain railway runs mid-May–late September from St Wolfgang to the top of Schafberg (www.schafbergbahn.at). Seats sell out so you should buy your tickets in advance, either at the ticket office or online (note that if you're planning to return to St Wolfgang on the Schafbergbahn instead of walking, you need to specify the time of your return journey at the time you book your ticket). Combo tickets are available for the Schafbergbahn and ferry, giving a slight saving, but are only sold as return tickets.

There is also a cable car which runs from beside the bus station at St Gilgen to the top of Zwölferhorn (1476m) (open all year, www.zwoe lferhorn.at).

ACCOMMODATION

- **Fuschl am See** (Fuschlsee, Walks 1–3): Landhotel Schützenhof (www.schuetzenhof.com).
- **St Gilgen** (Wolfgangsee, Walks 4–7): Gasthof zur Post (https://gasthofzurpost.at), Hotel Schernthaner (www.hotel-schern thaner.at).
- **St Lorenz** (Mondsee, Walk 8): Pension-Seecamp Nussbaumer (www.nussbaumer-mondsee. com), less than 100m from the bus stop and right by the lake, with its own lovely swimming spot; Gasthof Drachenwand (www.drachenwand.at).

There is also a wide choice of accommodation in Mondsee.

TOURIST INFORMATION

- Fuschlsee https://fuschlsee. salzkammergut.at/
- Wolfgangsee https://wolfgangsee. salzkammergut.at/
- Mondsee-Irrsee https://mondsee. salzkammergut.at/

WALK 1

Fuschlsee circuit

Start/finish	Fuschl am See (Landhotel Schützenhof)
Distance	11.5km
Ascent/descent	390m
Grade	Easy
Time	3hr
Terrain	A very easy lakeside path, with some sections along 4x4 tracks
Maximum altitude	714m
Maps	Kompass no. 229 Salzkammergut Sheet 1 (1:50,000)
Refreshments	Schloss Fuschl Fischerei (tel +43 (0)6229 2253); plenty of places to eat in Fuschl am See
Transport	Bus no. 150 to Fuschl am See

This beautiful circular walk around Fuschlsee makes for an easy half-day stroll, which can be combined with a walk on Ellmaustein (Walk 2). The route is described here going anticlockwise, but could just as easily be walked in a clockwise direction (walking clockwise, it's 50min from Fuschl am See to Schloss Fuschl).

▶ From Landhotel Schützenhof in Fuschl am See go S on Dorfstraße briefly then take a path on the R which brings you out onto the waterfront promenade. Follow the promenade N past the pizzeria, guesthouses and beaches, then turn L along a marked path behind some houses. The trail passes some beaches before bearing R and uphill slightly on a 4x4 track, marked 'seeweg', about 1hr from Fuschl-am-see. The path straight ahead follows the lakeside past several private beaches and boathouses before turning uphill to meet the 4x4 track.

Bear R onto an asphalt road on the edge of **Hundsmarkt**, then turn L onto another asphalt road which becomes a track. Bear R again, going past a path on your

To reach Landhotel Schützenhof from the bus station in Fuschl am See, walk N on Kirchenstraße then L (W) along Dorfstraße.

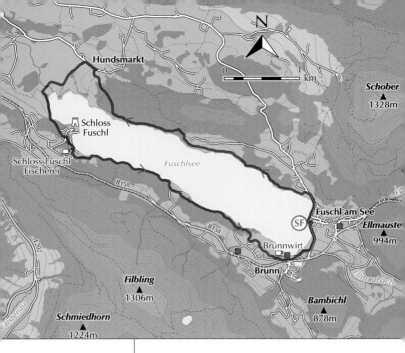

L leading across a marshy area, to arrive at the shallow outset stream of the lake (the Fuschler Ache), where there's a lone bench. Cross the stream, then go L past the café and playground by a beach (access only possible by buying a ticket). Follow the road S then bear R and slightly uphill, to the R of the castle (**Schloss Fuschl**). When you reach the asphalt road on the far side of the castle, go straight across and down some steps, before turning R onto an asphalt road beside the lake, which takes you to **Schloss Fuschl Fischerei**, which makes an excellent stop for lunch, 2hr from Fuschl am See.

The **Schloss Fuschl smokery** (open daily Apr–Mar, 08.00–18.00) has benches outside by the lake. The smoked trout sandwiches with horseradish sauce are worth doing the walk for in themselves. Schloss Fuschl itself was built in the 15th century as a hunting lodge of the Prince-Archbishops of Salzburg (and during World War 2 became the summer residence of the Foreign Minister of Nazi Germany, Joachim von Ribbentrop); it's now an upmarket hotel.

Continue along the asphalt road, which leads off to the R, then go L on a path beside the lake. Pass a path on the R marked Filbling (not the same route as described in Walk 3). The trail swings R away from the lake, and follows a lane with good views of Schober on the far side of the lake, to the NE. Pass the trail to Filbling (Walk 3) on your R, then go past a café, and up to the main road. Turn L on the main road past the **Brunnwirt** restaurant and bus stop, then take a path on your L and follow a lane parallel to the lake. Go R beside the stream, then L onto the main road which you follow past the car park to reach Landhotel Schützenhof in **Fuschl am See**.

Sunset on Fuschlsee from Fuschl am See

WALK 2
Ellmaustein from Fuschl am See

Start/finish	Fuschl am See (bus station)
Distance	6.5km
Ascent/descent	485m
Grade	Easy
Time	2hr 15min
Terrain	A short section on asphalt roads, then easy forest paths and 4x4 tracks
Maximum altitude	994m (Ellmaustein)
Maps	Fuschlseeregion (1:37,000), free from the local tourist office; Kompass no. 229 Salzkammergut Sheet 1 (1:50,000)
Refreshments	Several places to eat along the waterfront in Fuschl am See
Transport	Bus no. 150 to Fuschl am See

An easy hill just east of Fuschl am See, Ellmaustein has excellent views over Fuschlsee from the summit. It can easily be combined with Walk 1 on the same day (in which case, it makes sense to do Walk 2 first, in the morning, to avoid the possibility of afternoon cloud reducing the view, then go on to do Walk 1 afterwards, or in the afternoon).

Ellmaustein (994m) has clear views along the length of Fuschlsee, including Filbling (Walk 3) on the L.

From the bus station in Fuschl am See, go N on Kirchenstraße then E along Oberdorfstraße. Turn R along a drive after Elmauen Guesthouse, and cross the main road (care is needed as there is no crossing), before continuing S on an asphalt road next to Steakhouse Fuschl. After following this road for 15min, turn L onto a marked path which leads upwards through forest. Continue along a forestry track, bearing R, then go L on a path, and L again after crossing the forestry track, after which the path leads over a slight rise then down slightly to the large cross on Ellmaustein, 1hr after leaving the asphalt road. ◄

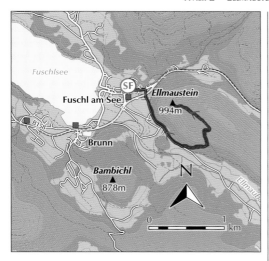

Descend to **Fuschl am See** by the same route (allow 1hr), taking care not to miss the turnoff on the R, from the forestry track onto the path.

Ellmaustein

WALK 3
Filbling from Fuschl am See

Start/finish	Fuschl am See (Landhotel Schützenhof)
Distance	10km
Ascent/descent	745m
Grade	Easy-Medium
Time	4hr 30min
Terrain	A short section on asphalt then mostly along 4x4 roads, with a steep final 30min of forest path
Maximum altitude	1307m (Filbling)
Maps	Fuschlseeregion (1:37,000), free from the local tourist office; Kompass no. 229 Salzkammergut Sheet 1 (1:50,000)
Refreshments	Several places to eat along the waterfront in Fuschl am See
Transport	Bus no. 150 to Fuschl am See (for a slightly shorter version, get off the no. 150 at the Oberbrunn bus stop)

An easy route to the prominent, narrow ridge on the south side of Fuschlsee, with breathtaking views. Filbling makes for a considerably easier hike than the better-known Schober on the north side of the lake (which has an exposed section secured by cables), and sees fewer hikers. The route also includes Filblingsee, a small lake surrounded by forest just below the saddle from which the trail leads up to the summit ridge.

A slightly more direct route is to simply follow Dorfstraße to the main road (B158) and turn R along this as far as the Oberbrunn bus stop.

From the bus station in Fuschl am See, walk N on Kirchenstraße then L (W) along Dorfstraße to reach Landhotel Schützenhof, and follow the road round to the L past the car park. Turn R just after crossing the Ellmaubach, following the lakeside trail (Walk 1) in reverse. ◀ Follow a path up to the main road, turn R past the **Brunnwirt** restaurant and bus stop, then go R again and bear right, passing alongside Restaurant Holzknechtstube. About 15min from Landhotel

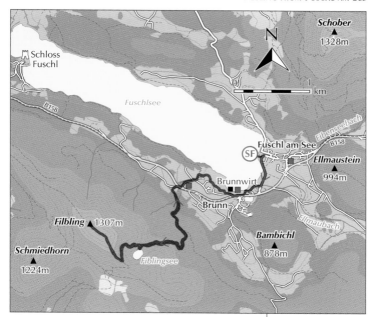

Schützenhof, just after passing a playground on your R, look out for the sign to Filbling on your L, following a 4x4 road past a house with a small spire on the roof, to reach the main road (**B158**) by the Oberbrunn bus stop. Cross the main road and turn R, then after crossing the bridge turn L, to reach a 4x4 track on your L signposted to Filbling.

Follow the 4x4 track up through forest, quite steep in places. At 1hr 10min after leaving the main road, you arrive at a path on your L which leads down in a minute or two to **Filblingsee**, where there's a picnic table and a small A-frame wooden shelter.

Return to the 4X4 track and follow this uphill to the saddle, then follow the trail on your R which climbs steeply up through forest (the sign marks Filbling as 1hr away, which on my visit had been crossed out and

53

Hiking along the ridge near the summit of Filbling

changed to 30min – the latter is the correct timing). The path is rocky and knotted with tree roots, and goes over a false summit before emerging on a narrow, grassy ridge, with spectacular views down over Fuschlsee, to reach the summit cross on **Filbling**, 45min from Fiblingsee.

> **Filbling** (1307m) has excellent views over Fuschlsee to Schober, the undulating ridge of which stretches east to become the Drachenwand and Almkogel (Walk 8), and to Schafberg further to the east.

> Descend by the same route to **Fuschl am See** (allow 2hr for the return).

WALK 4

*Plombergstein from
St Gilgen*

Start/finish	St Gilgen (Mozartplatz)
Distance	5km
Ascent/descent	455m
Grade	Easy-medium
Time	2hr 30min
Terrain	An easy walk on forest paths, with a rocky section which can be avoided; a short section on asphalt at the start
Maximum altitude	814m (Plombergstein)
Maps	Fuschlseeregion (1:37,000), free from the local tourist office; Kompass no. 229 Salzkammergut Sheet 1 (1:50,000)
Refreshments	St Gilgen
Transport	Bus no. 150 to St Gilgen

Few short hikes in Salzkammergut offer such a payoff as this easy walk to Plombergstein, a dome-like rock outcrop above St Gilgen with lovely views over Wolfgangsee from the top, and a labyrinthine area of shattered rocks and boulders called the Steinklüft.

From Mozartplatz in St Gilgen, walk N along Steinklüftstraße (signposted to Plombergstein), which leads out of town with views of Plombergstein ahead, and up to the main road. Go straight ahead over the main road (B154) and up a minor road, then where this bends R (towards Obenau and Almkogel, Walk 8) go straight ahead on a forest track. Where the trail splits into three, take the middle path. ▶ Climb gradually uphill with a stream descending on your L. Turn L onto an asphalt road then L onto a path again at the bend. Cross the stream on a footbridge, go uphill and bear R, passing a trail on your L.

The trail on the L also leads to Plombergstein, but is a less interesting route.

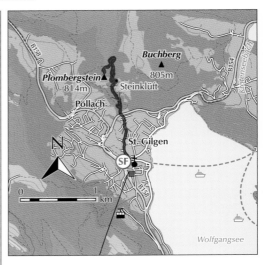

At 30min from Mozartplatz you reach a junction, where you bear R then immediately L through a cleft in the rock, marked by red arrows. (The path straight ahead from the junction simply detours the Steinklüft.) This is the **Steinklüft**, where the trail winds through a rather wonderful mass of huge, moss-covered boulders, ducking into hidden caves and squeezing between rocks and on the far side, going through a narrow, steep-walled gorge. ◄ At the far end of the gorge, the path continues N and uphill to reach a huge, almost perfectly symmetrical block of stone at the base of a cliff, near some rock climbing routes. After squeezing through a narrow gap between a chunk of rock and the cliff face, the path leads further uphill, turning sharply L to reach a saddle, where you bear L and ascend to the top of **Plombergstein**, 1hr 30min from St Gilgen, where a privately owned hut sits on a broad terrace overlooking Wolfgangsee.

During the Napoleonic Wars, locals used the Steinklüft as a hiding place for their valuables.

Plombergstein has picture-perfect views across Wolfgangsee, including the Bleckwand and the

Near Steinklüft, on the Plombergstein hiking trail

prominent, lop-sided Sparber rising above the southeast corner of the lake. According to legend, three princes set out from Salzburg to find the most beautiful view in the world, with the promise that the one who succeeded in this task would win the hand of the king's daughter. However, on arriving at this point overlooking Wolfgangsee, they were so captivated by the view that they turned to stone, remaining here forever as Plombergstein, Mitterstein and Obenauerstein.

Descend by the same route to **St Gilgen** (allow 1hr).

WALK 5
Zwölferhorn

Start	Zwölferhorn upper cable car station
Finish	St Gilgen (Mozartplatz)
Distance	8.5km
Ascent	285m
Descent	1185m
Grade	Easy
Time	3hr 40min
Terrain	Broad, easy, mostly level paths for the Pillstein Panorama Circuit; followed by descent on sometimes steep forest paths and 4x4 tracks
Maximum altitude	1522m (Zwölferhorn)
Maps	Kompass no. 229 Salzkammergut Sheet 1 (1:50,000)
Refreshments	Arnika Hütte (www.arnika12.at); Franzl's Hütte (www.franzlshuette.at); Sausteigalm; Berggasthof Weisswand (www.weisswand.at)
Transport	Bus no. 150 to St Gilgen

This easy walk includes the Pillstein Panorama Circuit, and the hike downhill to St Gilgen, which passes some nice huts. For a shorter walk take the cable car down.

From the upper cable car station on Zwölferhorn, walk uphill (S) to the summit of **Zwölferhorn**, with its large cross and extensive views. Go over the top and down the crest of a rocky ridge, then straight ahead along a gravel track. Pass **Arnika Hütte** (open late May–end October, closed Tuesdays), and bear L where the 4x4 track splits. After 10min from Arnika Hütte bear L on a broad path, or for enhanced views follow the slightly higher path just to the L of this, and slightly further ahead go up over **Pillsteinhöhe** (1478m), the raised hillock to the R of the trail.

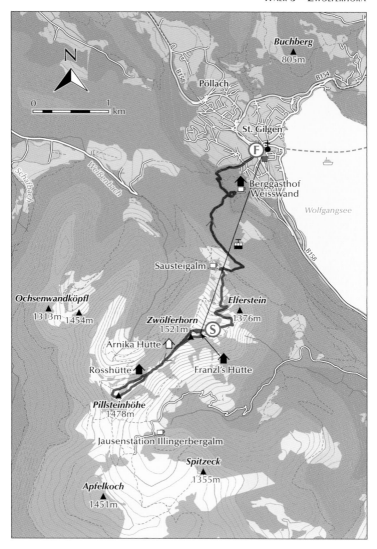

View south on the Pillstein Panorama Circuit, Zwölferhorn

Pillsteinhöhe is topped with a cross. A bench beside the trail here has sweeping views of the mountains to the south and southwest, including the Gennerhorn to the west-southwest, recognisable by the distinctive 'bump' on its ridge – and, further away to the southwest, the Berchtesgaden Alps straddling the border with Germany, among these the Hoher Göll and Watzmann.

Follow the trail around to the R, passing the diminutive **Rosshütte** on your L beside a small pond. Pass the junction with your outgoing route, then after passing Arnika Hütte again bear L around the N slopes of Zwölferhorn, to arrive at **Franzl's Hütte** (open May–October, food and accommodation) and the upper cable car station beyond, 1hr 30min after starting out on the circuit.

Follow the path down in front of Franzl's Hütte, then bear R and go under the cable car, contouring the hillside to reach a junction on the saddle between Zwölferhorn and Elferstein. Go L here (not NE down the ridge to

Elferstein), following the ski run before turning R and taking a steep shortcut down through the forest. After 1hr from Franzl's Hütte, arrive at **Sausteigalm** (1110m, open from mid May–late October, daily in July/August otherwise closed Tuesdays). Bear R along the 4x4 track, passing a small wayside shrine on your R, then go L and follow the 4x4 track down through forest.

At 40min from Sausteigalm you arrive at a junction, with the very pleasant **Berggasthof Weisswand** (780m, open May–October, food and accommodation) just 1min down a path in front of you, its broad terrace commanding beautiful views over **Wolfgangsee**. Follow the 4x4 road L (NW) from the junction, then take a path on your R marked St Gilgen Waldweg, passing a trail on your L marked Mozart-steig. Go straight ahead onto asphalt to arrive back at the main road in front of the lower cable car station in **St Gilgen**, a little over 2hr from Franzl's Hütte.

'Cable car on Zwölferhorn, overlooking St Gilgen and Wolfgansee

WALK 6

St Wolfgang to St Gilgen via Falkenstein

Start	St Wolfgang
Finish	St Gilgen (Mozartplatz)
Distance	9km
Ascent	495m
Descent	495m
Grade	Easy
Time	2hr 30min
Terrain	An easy path through forest and alongside the lake
Maximum altitude	795m
Maps	Kompass no. 229 Salzkammergut Sheet 1 (1:50,000)
Refreshments	Gasthof-Hotel Fürberg (www.fuerberg.com); St Gilgen
Transport	By ferry from St Gilgen to St Wolfgang via Fürberg (www. schafbergbahn.at); otherwise bus no. 546 from Strobl to St Wolfgang

An easy walk along the pilgrimage route between St Gilgen and St Wolfgang (there is no road along this steep stretch of shoreline between Ried and Fürberg). It visits the church at Falkenstein, which is said to have been founded by St Wolfgang in the 10th century.

From the waterfront in St Wolfgang by the ferry jetty and the Schafbergbahn station, walk N up Schafbergbahnstraße and L along Sternallee which after crossing the stream becomes Obere Riederstraße. Follow the asphalt road W through the settlement of Ried, bearing R after 15min.

Turn R at an electric tower and R again at a small private chapel (which belongs to a local farmstead), following an asphalt path uphill. Keep straight ahead on a gravel track, cross a stream and bear R, with a waterfall on your R. After 45min from St Wolfgang go L at a small shelter, on a trail marked 'Aberseeblick'. The trail leads

uphill over knotted tree roots to arrive at a good **view-point** in 10min. Return to the shelter on the main track and turn L, keeping straight ahead past a trail on your R. Pass a white chapel on your L, then follow the path downhill into a clearing, with **Falkenstein church** built into a cliff on your L.

Falkenstein pilgrimage trail

> According to legend St Wolfgang, the 10th century bishop of Regensburg, came to live as a hermit at **Falkenstein church** (having supposedly chosen the spot by throwing an axe, and building a church where it landed), and during the medieval period the place become an important pilgrimage site. The two hollows in the wall are said to have been where he slept, and the spring in a nearby building was supposedly created when St Wolfgang struck the rock with his staff, in order to give water to a monk who was there with him.

Station of the cross on the Falkenstein pilgrimage trail

Continue downhill beyond the church, passing another Aberseeblick trail on your L, to arrive on the shore of **Wolfgangsee** in 20min. Turn R along the waterfront to reach the ferry jetty at **Fürberg** in 10min, opposite Gasthof-Hotel Fürberg (542m, open mid May–mid

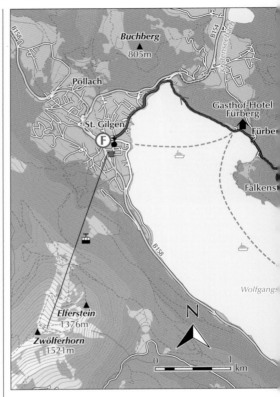

Sparber and other peaks rising above Wolfgangsee, viewed from St Gilgen

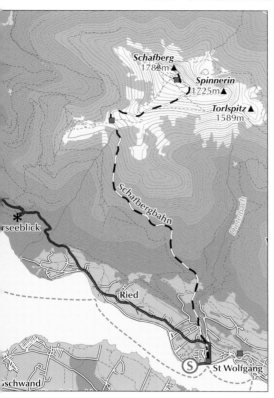

October, daily in July/August otherwise closed Tuesdays, a highly regarded restaurant). ▶ Bear L and follow an asphalt road (Mondseestraße) into **St Gilgen**, bearing R just before reaching the ferry jetty to arrive at Mozartplatz in the town centre.

The lakeside path is particularly pretty beyond this point, right by the water's edge and overhung with trees.

65

WALK 7

Schafberg to Fürberg and St Gilgen

Start	Schafbergbahn upper station
Finish	St Gilgen
Distance	10km
Ascent	130m
Descent	1360m
Grade	Medium
Time	3hr 20min
Terrain	Clear paths over grassy slopes, then steep forest paths
Maximum altitude	1782m (Schafberg)
Maps	Kompass no. 229 Salzkammergut Sheet 1 (1:50,000); there's a handy diagram of the routes on Schafberg (not suitable for route finding) on the Schafbergbahn website (www.schafbergbahn.at/).
Refreshments	Berghotel Schafbergspitz (http://schafberg.net/) and Himmelspforthütte (1760m, open mid May–late September) both on the summit of Schafberg; however, note that Gasthof Schafbergalpe is closed; numerous places in St Wolfgang and St Gilgen.
Transport	The Schafbergbahn (www.schafbergbahn.at) runs mid-May–late September from St Wolfgang to Schafbergalm and on to Shafbergspitz station just below the summit. Seats sell out so you should buy your tickets in advance (see section introduction). (Note that if you're planning to return to St Wolfgang on the Schafbergbahn instead of walking, you need to specify your return time when you book your ticket). To get to St Wolfgang from St Gilgen, take the ferry (www.schafbergbahn.at) via Fürberg. Otherwise, bus no. 546 to St Wolfgang, and bus no. 150 from St Gilgen.

One of the most striking and easily recognisable mountains in the area, Schafberg (1782m) towers over the north shore of Wolfgangsee, its lopsided dorsal fin of a summit easy to pick out among surrounding peaks from far across Salzkammergut. Its southern slopes rise steeply through forest to open pasture; its north face falls in a sheer cliff almost 400m. Schafberg is also famous for its vintage mountain railway, the Schafbergbahn, a ride up on which is included in this walk.

There are several hiking routes on Schafberg. The nicest part for hiking is the section between the summit and upper railway station, and the Schafbergalm railway station. After this it's a steep descent through forest, either to St Wolfgang (path 23), or to Fürberg and St Gilgen (path 804) as described here. There's also a more difficult route from the upper railway station to St Wolfgang, which goes through the Himmelspforte and down (exposed, cables) to Suissensee, below Schafberg's north face, then on via Mittersee and Törlspitz (exposed, cables) to Mönichsee and path 25.

The historic **Schafbergbahn** is the steepest cog railway in Austria. Opened in 1893, it reaches a maximum gradient of 26% on its nearly-6km route from the shore of Wolfgangsee at 542m, to a station at 1732m, just 50m below the summit of Schafberg. The trains stop briefly at Dorneralm (1015m) for the locomotives to refill water tanks, and Schafbergalm

Schafbergbahn approaching Schafbergalm

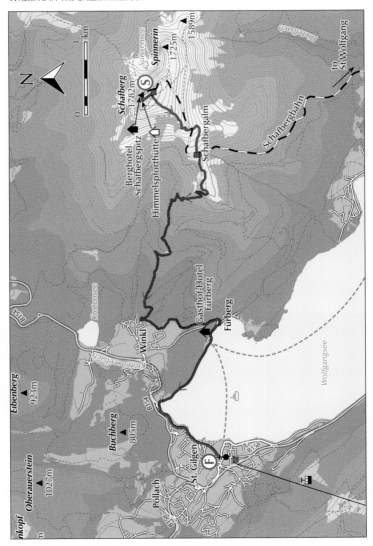

(1363m) to pick up or set down passengers. The fleet consists of five vintage, coal-fired steam locomotives (built in 1893 and 1894); four modern, oil-powered steam locomotives (built in 1992 and 1995); one vintage diesel railcar (built in 1964); and two diesel-electric locomotives (built in 2010 and 2016); it's generally the modern oil-powered locomotives which do the hauling these days.

From the upper Schafbergbahn station walk up to the summit of **Schafberg** (1782m) behind the busy **Berghotel Schafbergspitz** (open May–late September, food and accommodation), with astonishingly good views from the clifftop path above the sheer north face – over Fuschlsee, Mondsee, Irsee and Attersee on one side, and Wolfgangsee on the other.

From the summit of **Schafberg** there are clear views of the Höllengebirge (Walks 11 and 12) to the northeast, Almkogel (Walk 8) and the Drachenwand to the northwest, and Dachstein and the Gosaukamm (Walks 24–30) to the southeast. The high plateau to the southwest is the Tennen Gebirge, and to the right of this beyond the Zwölferhorn (Walk 5) you can see the Berchtesgaden Alps, which sprawl across the border with Germany.

Return to the upper railway station, cross the tracks and go straight ahead downhill, passing a trail on your L to Mönichsee and crossing the tracks again further down (good for photos if there's a train on its way up). Some 15min brings you to **Schafbergalm**, where a bridge crosses the railway line. Pass the old Gasthof Schafbergalpe (closed) and follow a good track leading W to a junction, where you turn R on a 4x4 track heading N, signposted to Winkl (all signposts on this path are to Winkl, not St Gilgen). ▶

Follow a path leading steeply downhill through forest, then go L onto a 4x4 road then R onto a path off this, and straight ahead over another 4x4 road, 1hr from the

The 4x4 track going straight ahead leads down to St Wolfgang in 2hr.

Sparber and other peaks rising above Wolfgangsee, viewed from St Gilgen

It is signposted 'St Gilgen wanderweg' – don't follow the sign to St Gilgen on the R, which leads along the road.

junction with the trail to St Wolfgang. Bear L at the next 4x4 road, then R down a path, to arrive on the outskirts of **Winkl**, 2hr from Schafbergalm.

Turn L onto an asphalt road, then straight ahead on a path which leads along the edge of a field then bear L. ◀ At the far end of the field go L on a broad, level forest trail, beside a stream. Go L onto the asphalt road, then bear L to reach the welcome shore of **Wolfgangsee**. Turn R and follow the lakeside to Gasthof Fürberg and the **Fürberg** ferry jetty, just over 20min from Winkl.

Continue along a beautiful, broad lakeside path, overhung with trees. Bear L and follow an asphalt road (Mondseestraße) into **St Gilgen**, bearing R just before reaching the ferry jetty to arrive at Mozartplatz in the town centre, 30min from Fürberg.

WALK 8

Almkogel and Eibensee from St Lorenz

Start/finish	St Lorenz (Gries bus stop)
Distance	12km
Ascent/descent	950m
Grade	Medium–difficult
Time	5hr
Terrain	Forest trail, quite steep in places, with a short section on asphalt at the beginning of the route; from Almkogel to Eibensee the route follows a 4x4 track.
Maximum altitude	1130m (4x4 road on Höllkar)
Maps	Naturerlebniskarte Mondseeland (1:35,000); Kompass no. 229 Salzkammergut Sheet 1 (1:50,000)
Refreshments	Pension-Seecamp Nussbaumer (www.nussbaumer-mondsee.com); Gasthof Drachenwand (www.drachenwand.at)
Transport	Bus no. 156 runs between St Gilgen (connecting with bus no. 150) and Mondsee via St Lorenz – get off at the Gries bus stop

Unlike the nearby Drachenwand, the route to Almkogel is a straightforward hiking trail, steep in places but with none of the exposed via ferrata sections associated with routes on its more famous neighbour. There are superb views from the summit to the Drachenwand and across the expanse of Mondsee. The route has been extended here to include Eibensee, a small, secluded lake west of Almkogel.

From the Gries bus stop in St Lorenz, follow an asphalt road W from the main road, and turn right onto another asphalt road at the junction, passing a small chapel on your L. In just over 5min turn L on an asphalt road, opposite house number 53 and before reaching **Gasthof Drachenwand** (open Wednesday–Friday for lunch, Saturday and Sunday for lunch and dinner, food and

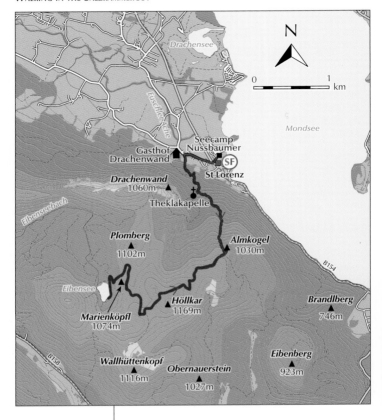

accommodation), then continue along the marked 4x4 track into the forest.

Pass a trail on your R leading to Schober (a slightly more difficult peak above Fuschlsee, 3h 30min away) and Ruine Wartenfels (the ruins of a 13th century castle on the flanks of Schober, 2h 30min away). Then 15min after leaving the asphalt road reach a small **chapel** (Theklakapelle). ◄ Cross the footbridge over the stream (don't take the path on the R, which leads towards the

The chapel was undergoing repairs in 2019.

Drachenwand), and begin ascending steadily on a winding forest path, at times narrow and fairly steep. After 1h 20min from the footbridge, gain a saddle and turn L to reach the summit of **Almkogel** (1030m).

> The rocky summit of **Almkogel** pokes out above the trees with sheer drops on two sides, with a metal cross, and spectacular views over Mondsee to the east and the Drachenwand to the northwest.

Return to the saddle, where a trail on the L descends to Plombergstein (Walk 4) and St Gilgen via Obenauer. Unless you want to shorten the walk (in which case, turn R and return to St Lorenz by the same route), continue straight ahead on a path signposted to Eibensee, then turn R onto a 4x4 road. Follow this as it climbs gently uphill across the shoulder of **Höllkar** (1169m), then descends again in a couple of long switchbacks. ▶ The 4x4 road descends more steeply after rounding the next corner (you can see the small cross at Kleines Marienköpfl above you on your L), then 1h from Almkogel you reach a footpath on your L which leads down to **Eibensee**. Follow the path along the shore of the lake, to the small beach at the

You will pass a trail to Kleines Marienköpfl, a viewpoint about 15min away, on your L.

On the trail to Almkogel from St Gilgen

View across Mondsee from St Lorenz

far end, where there's a lone bench, and a small wooden A-frame shelter.

Return along the 4x4 road to the saddle below Almkogel (1hr), then turn L and follow the path back down to **St Lorenz** (another 1hr 20min).

Traunkirchen, Traunsee

Traunsee is the deepest lake in Austria (191m), and the second largest in Salzkammergut after Attersee. Despite stretching up to the northern boundary of the Salzkammergut region, beyond which the land immediately becomes much flatter, the lake is nevertheless surrounded by some huge mountains. Traunstein (1691m), on the east shore of the lake, is one of the most striking peaks in Salzkammergut, while above the southwest corner of the lake, the Höllengebirge – a high karst plateau on a slightly smaller scale than Dachstein or the Totes Gebirge – stretches around 11km over towards the shore of Attersee.

There are some outstandingly good hikes on the Höllengebirge, including the popular Alberfeldkogel (1707m, Walk 11) and the higher, more remote Grosser Höllkogel (1862m, Walk 12). Further rugged peaks stand on the southeast corner of the lake, including Erlakogel (1575m). Two beautiful lakes lie tucked below the north slopes of the Höllengebirge, Vorderer and Hinterer Langbathsee (Walk 10); another small lake, Laudachsee, lies on the northeast side of Traunstein, easily accessible from Grünberg, the mountain above Gmunden (Walk 9). Further to the southeast, Offensee has a wonderful setting below the northern edge of the Totes Gebirge, and is the kicking off point for hikes up onto the Totes Gebirge itself (Walk 15).

The two main towns on Traunsee are Gmunden in the north, and Ebensee in the south – Gmunden being well placed for hikes on Grünberg, but Ebensee being the best base for most of the other hikes around the lake, including those described here.

South from Traunsee on the River Traun, the elegant spa town of **Bad Ischl**, which for many years was the summer residence of Emperor Franz Josef I and his wife Sisi, lies at the centre of the Salzkammergut region, on the main rail and bus routes, and it's almost certain that you'll pass through Bad Ischl at some point. There are some very good hiking routes around the town, including Katrin (1542m, Walk 14), the Hohe Schrott (1839m) and Zimnitz (1745m), as well as the very easy Ewige Wand (Walk 15) further south.

TRANSPORT

Gmunden, Ebensee and Bad Ischl are all on the railway line between Attnang-Puchheim and Obertraun (timetables at www.oebb.at). For Ebensee, make sure you get out at Ebensee Landungplatz station, not the one just called Ebensee which is actually further away from the town.

The Feuerkogel Seilbahn (www.feuerkogel.info) runs from the outskirts of Ebensee up to 1592m; the lower cable car station is a 15-minute walk from Ebensee Landungplatz, on the road towards Langbathsee.

Ferries run the length of Traunsee connecting Gmunden, Altmünster,

Hoisn, Traunkirchen and Ebensee several times a day (timetables at www.traunseeschifffahrt.at). Bus no. 505 also runs between Gmunden and Ebensee (timetables at www.postbus.at).

There is no public transport to Offensee (Walk 13). However, Traunsee Taxi run a shuttle service between Ebensee and the car park on the E shore of Offensee (Parkplatz Ost) between 0700 and 2000 (Line 41, departing Ebensee railway station or Feuerkogel lower cable car station, one-way fare €6, tel +43 (0)50 422 422). You need to call at least 1hr ahead to book, preferably earlier (they can get fully booked during the summer with other routes).

- **Ebensee** (Walks 9–13): Gasthof Roitner (Langbathstraße 74, tel +43 (0)6133 20630, www.booking.com/hotel/at/gasthof-roitner.en-gb.html) is an excellent small guesthouse 10min on foot from the train station, near the Feuerkogel cable car station, very good value, with delicious evening meals and a huge breakfast; Hotel Post (www.hotel-post-ebensee.at) is another good choice.

- **Bad Ischl** (Walks 14–15): Pension Waldesruh (Kaltenbachstraße 43, tel +43 (0)699 1187 6994, https://pensionwaldesruh.com/).

There are several huts offering accommodation near Feuerkogel Seilbahn upper cable car station including Feuerkogelhaus (www.feuerkogel.com).

- Traunsee-Almtal Tourist Office Hauptstraße 34, Ebensee/Toscanapark 1, Gmunden https://traunsee-almtal.salzkammergut.at/
- Bad Ischl Tourist Office Auböckplatz 5/Trinkhalle https://badischl.salzkammergut.at/

View across Traunsee, with Traunstein on the left, from the waterfront at Ebensee (Walks 9–12)

WALK 9
Grünberg and Laudachsee

Start	Gmunden (Rathausplatz)
Finish	Hoisn (ferry jetty)
Distance	13.5km
Ascent	780m
Descent	780m
Grade	Easy–medium
Time	5hr
Terrain	Forest trail, steep in places, and 4x4 roads
Maximum altitude	984m (Grünberg)
Maps	Ferienregion Traunsee (1:50,000); Kompass no. 229 Salzkammergut Sheet 2 (1:50,000)
Refreshments	Grünberg Alm (https://gruenberg.info/); Ramsaualm (www.laudachsee.com); Gasthof-Hotel Hoisnwirt (www.hoisnwirt.at)
Transport	Traunsee ferry from Goisn to Gmunden or Ebensee (www.traunseeschifffahrt.at); train to Gmunden from Ebensee; there's also a cable car on Grünberg (https://gruenberg.info/en/)

An easy hike up Gmunden's popular local 'hill', Grünberg, continuing to Laudachsee, a beautiful lake on the north flanks of Traunstein, then descending to Hoisn and returning to Gmunden by ferry. It's also possible to take the cable car up to Grünberg.

From the main square (Rathausplatz) in Gmunden, walk E along the waterfront and cross the bridge over the Traun, then turn R and follow the lakeside promenade past the marina and small park. Turn R along Traunsteinstraße then turn L on Ackerweg (the first street on the L after the street leading to the cable car station).

Keep straight ahead, following the road uphill, then go up a flight of steps (signposted Laudachsee) and along

a path beside a fence. Turn L on a path which ascends steeply through the forest by way of wooden steps, going straight ahead across a mountain bike track and following the signs to Grünberg (not R which is marked Laudachsee). The trail becomes steeper again before levelling out a bit onto a gravel track, going through clearings and under the cable car route, with a rail-mounted summer toboggan run on your L to reach the top of **Grünberg** (984m), 2hr 30min from Gmunden. ▶

If you're walking with children, good luck getting past the toboggan run in a hurry!

There's a restaurant on **Grünberg** (Grünberg Alm, open daily), above a playground, and a viewing platform beside the upper cable car station. There's also a treetop walk culminating in a 39m high viewing tower, and the summer toboggan run – so it can get quite busy here in the summer.

Follow the well-used gravel track E past the upper cable car station and the huge viewing tower at the end of the treetop walk, then after 20min turn R off the track, onto a path which leads downhill through the forest. At a junction, go R and then L on a gravel 4x4 road. Partway along this, pass a **spring** on your L.

The spring, where the water pours from seven elaborately wrought faucets, each with a crown, refers to the legend of the **Sieben Brunnlein** (seven little fountains). Legend tells that a witch turned the seven sons of a wicked king hereabouts into seven fountains to punish him.

Laudachsee, with Katzenstein beyond

Just over 1hr from Grünberg, arrive at the **Ramsaualm** restaurant (open March– end of October) with **Laudachsee** spread below on your left.

> **Laudachsee** sits in a beautiful setting among meadows, below the craggy summit of Katzenstein. A trail leads south from Laudachsee, over the saddle between Katzenstein and Traunstein, to reach Moaralm; however, the route is more difficult than the trail described here.

Retrace your steps back along the 4x4 road past the spring to the junction, and go straight ahead (marked Hoisn), then turn L down a path through the forest. Cross a 4x4 track twice, keeping straight ahead on the path each time, then go straight ahead on a 4x4 track (not R), then L down a steep path. Cross a bridge over a stream and turn L on a 4x4 road, then turn R onto a path, and R again onto another 4x4 road. Bear L where this forks, go over a streambed (dry in summer), then straight ahead on a path downhill. Turn L at the asphalt road then R to reach the waterfront at **Hoisn**, with the ferry jetty in front of you and **Gasthof-Hotel Hoisnwirt** (open early March– end of October, food and accommodation, reckoned to be one of the best places to eat around Gmunden) on your L, 1hr 30min from Laudachsee.

WALK 10
Vorderer and Hinterer Langbathsee

Start/finish	Vorderer Langbathsee (car park)
Distance	7km
Ascent/descent	80m
Grade	Easy
Time	2hr
Terrain	Very easy lakeside walk on broad, mostly level 4x4 tracks.
Maximum altitude	755m
Maps	Ferienregion Traunsee (1:50,000); Kompass no. 229 Salzkammergut Sheet 2 (1:50,000)
Refreshments	Café at Vorderer Langbathsee car park
Transport	Traunsee Taxi run a shuttle service between Ebensee and Vorderer Langbathsee between 0700 and 2000 (Line 40, departing Ebensee railway station or Feurkogel lower cable car station, one-way fare €6, tel +43 (0)50 422 422). You need to call at least 1hr ahead to book, preferably earlier (they can get fully booked during the summer with other routes). Note there is no mobile signal at the lakes or along much of the Langbathtal, so you need to arrange your pickup time before leaving Ebensee. Otherwise, it's an 8km road walk back to Ebensee.

The twin lakes of Vorderer and Hinterer Langbathsee sit below the steep slopes of the Höllengebirge, at the head of the Langbathtal. The route is described here going clockwise, but it really makes no difference whether you choose to walk clockwise or anticlockwise. A longer and more challenging hike can be created by combining this lakeside walk with an ascent of Brunnkogel, the 1708m peak to the west of Hinterer Langbathsee; however, in the summer of 2019 the trail to Brunnkogel was closed due to rockfall.

From the car park, follow a broad, level track along the N shore of **Vorderer Langbathsee**. At the far (W) end of the lake keep straight ahead (the track on the L joins with

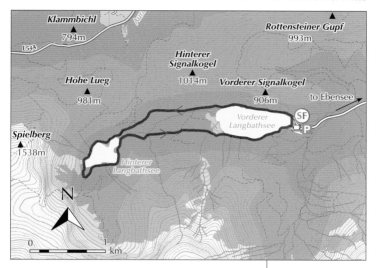

the return route) and follow the 4x4 track uphill , and around the shore of **Hinterer Langbathsee**, the surface of which is around 70m higher than the lower lake, with a breathtaking panorama of Brunnkogel and other rocky peaks of the Höllengebirge reflected in its waters below a ring of larches. Pass a trail to Brunnkogel at the far end of the lake, then return along the S shore of both lakes along broad tracks to the car park (where there is a **café**).

Vorderer Langbathsee

WALK 11
Feuerkogel, Alberfeldkogel and Helmeskogel

Start/finish	Feuerkogel Seilbahn (upper cable car station)
Distance	7.5km
Ascent/descent	440m
Grade	Medium
Time	3hr 30min
Terrain	Rocky, well-marked paths with a slightly exposed section near Alberfeldkogel
Maximum altitude	1705m (Alberfeldkogel)
Maps	Ferienregion Traunsee (1:50,000); Kompass no. 229 Salzkammergut Sheet 2 (1:50,000)
Refreshments	Several huts (with accommodation) near the upper cable car station, including Feuerkogelhaus (www.feuerkogel. com)
Transport	The Feuerkogel Seilbahn (www.feuerkogel.info) runs from the outskirts of Ebensee up to 1592m; the lower cable car station is a 10-minute walk from Hotel Post in Ebensee, on the road towards Langbathsee
Note	Several sections secured with rope (mild exposure)

A short hike between three peaks on the eastern edge of the Höllengebirge, a spectacular karst plateau high above the southern end of Traunsee and Attersee, with breathtaking views. Although technically speaking the name Feuerkogel refers to the 1592m peak crowned by the upper station of the Feuerkogel Seilbahn, it is also used more generally to refer to the surrounding area at this end of the Höllengebirge.

This walk makes use of the Feuerkogel cable car for both ascent and descent; however, it's possible to hike up to Feuerkogel from Ebensee instead, if preferred – the most direct route goes via Wimmersberg and Kranabethhütte and takes around 4hr; however, some of it is shared with a mountain bike route. Another route descends via Spitzalm to Langweis (5hr from the upper cable car station), but is less convenient if you're based in Ebensee or Gmunden.

A nicer choice if you want to hike up is to start from the road leading to Langbathsee (Walk 10) – the trail starts from Landgasthaus in der Kreh, and follows path no. 832 up to the upper cable car station. If you're hiking here in August, check the dates of the Feuerkogel-Berglauf (Feuerkogel Mountain Run), one of the largest mountain runs in Austria.

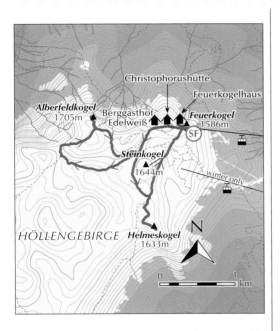

▸ Walk W from the Feuerkogel Seilbahn upper cable car station, passing the **Feuerkogelhaus guesthouse** and restaurant (open mid-May–end of October, food and accommodation) on your R, and following signs to Riederhütte. Keep straight ahead where a broad, well-used trail to Alberfeldkogel branches off to the R, to reach a junction with the trail to Helmeskogel (which you'll follow later). Turn R here (signposted Riederhütte and Hochleckenhaus), descending slightly at first, on an

Feuerkogel has the distinction of being the spot with the highest wind speeds ever recorded in Austria – a sobering 220kmh.

85

undulating, rocky path. The path leads up to join a rough 4x4 track briefly, before dropping down to the L again.

After 45min from the cable car station you arrive at a junction, where the trail to Riederhütte swings L (see Walk 12). Turn R here (marked Alberfeldkogel) and follow a path leading steeply uphill. The trail is slightly exposed in places, as it climbs above cliffs with sweeping views of Attersee and Langbathsee (Walk 10), before the cross on the summit of Alberfeldkogel comes into view ahead. Some 30min brings you to the broad, main trail which you passed earlier. Turn L onto this to reach the summit of **Alberfeldkogel** (1705m), with its huge metal cross, the Europakreuz, in 5min.

> The views from **Alberfeldkogel** are breathtaking, stretching across Traunsee to Traunstein and Gmunden, and the flatter countryside further north, and northwest across Langbathsee (Walk 10) to Attersee, while Alpine choughs hop about on the rocks above the cliff edge. A via ferrata route climbs below the east face of the summit.
>
> The 5m-high Europakreuz was installed in 2006 and is constructed of metal cubes, one

Europakreuz on Alberfeldkogel

for each EU member state at that time, each of which contains a chunk of rock from that country which tells a piece of its history. For example, the Austrian stone comes from a well-known quarry in Burgenland; the stone from Latvia comes from the base of the former Lenin monument in Riga, which was dismantled in August 1991; and the 'stone' from Germany is a fragment of the Berlin Wall. The metal cubes are open sided, symbolising the principles of free movement within the EU.

Descend on the main trail, keeping straight ahead past the path you came up on, and following the broad, well-used path downhill towards the cable car station (Seilbahn). Pass a trail on your left to Heumahdgupf, then 20min from Alberfeldkogel turn R on a path marked Kranabethhütte, descending gradually to join the rough 4x4 track encountered briefly earlier. Turn L along this to reach the junction with the trail to Helmeskogel, where you turn R on a broad, well-engineered track.

After 20min along the trail go straight ahead past a path on the L marked Karst- und Dolinen-Erlebnisweg (the Karst and Doline Adventure Trail, which you'll follow on your return), then after climbing steadily for a further 15min pass a large cross on your R, on the summit of **Helmeskogel** (1633m). The path continues beyond this for a few metres, across a narrow neck to a small viewing platform overlooking the Traun Valley, with views of Traunsee and Traunstein.

Descend following the same route as far as the Karst- und Dolinen-Erlebnisweg, and turn R onto this. (There a few sections on this trail secured with ropes, but it's only very mildly exposed and doesn't require any climbing gear. It's fine for kids too – I walked it with my eight-year-old daughter. If preferred, however, you can also just continue back to the cable car station following the same paths as on your outbound route instead.) The path weaves around a succession of dolines and other karst features, with information boards in German and English on how the surrounding landscape was formed, before

Descendng from Alberfeldkogel towards the trail to Helmeskogel

crossing some steeper slopes, where the trail is secured with rope in places. Around 35min brings you out of the Karst- und Dolinen-Erlebnisweg, at the bottom of the **Steinkogel chairlift**. Go downhill past this then up again to reach **Feuerkogelhaus** and the cable car station, 1hr from Helmeskogel.

WALK 12

Grosser Höllkogel and Riederhütte

Start/finish	Feuerkogel Seilbahn (upper cable car station)
Distance	9km
Ascent/descent	555m
Grade	Medium
Time	5hr
Terrain	Rocky mountain paths, steep in places. The karst terrain below the Grosser Höllkogel would be difficult to navigate in low visibility, so in case of poor weather take the more direct trail to Riederhütte instead. One slightly exposed section with steel cables.
Maximum altitude	1862m (Grosser Höllkogel)
Maps	Ferienregion Traunsee (1:50,000); Kompass no. 229 Salzkammergut Sheet 2 (1:50,000)
Refreshments	Riederhütte (www.alpenverein.at/riederhuette/); Feuerkogelhaus (www.feuerkogel.com)
Transport	The Feuerkogel Seilbahn (www.feuerkogel.info) runs from the outskirts of Ebensee up to 1592m; the lower cable car station is a 10-minute walk from Hotel Post in Ebensee, on the road towards Langbathsee.

This is a superb hike to the highest peak on the Höllengebirge, and the nearby Riederhütte. A longer route than Walk 11 to Alberfeldkogel and with fewer hikers, it passes through some spectacular karst terrain, and offers stupendous views south from the summit of the Grosser Höllkogel. Like Walk 11, this route makes use of the cable car for both ascent and descent from Ebensee (see the introduction to Walk 11 for information on hiking up instead of taking the cable car).

Walk W from the Feuerkogel upper cable car station on the same trail as Walk 11, following signs to Riederhütte and passing the Feuerkogelhaus guesthouse and restaurant on your R. Go straight ahead past a broad trail on your R

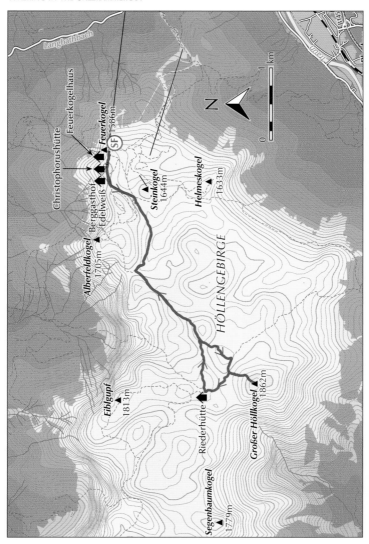

to Alberfeldkogel (Walk 11), then at a junction with the trail to Helmeskogel (Walk 11) turn R, onto an undulating, rocky path marked Riederhütte and Hochleckenhaus. The trail descends slightly at first, before climbing to a rough 4x4 track. Turn L along this, then follow the path where it drops down again on your L.

After 45min from the upper cable car station you pass another path on the R leading up towards Alberfeldkogel (Walk 11). Turn L here (signposted to Riederhütte) and follow a steep, rocky trail uphill, with views of **Helmeskogel** to the SE. The trail passes above a steep-sided doline, with the aid of steel cables (slightly exposed), then 1hr 30min from the upper cable car station you reach a junction with a path to Riederhütte on your R (by which you'll return).

Go straight ahead here, into a gully with increasingly impressive karst scenery, with the broad dome of the Grosser Höllkogel ahead of you. Turn R where the trail forks, then 45min from the Riederhütte turnoff go L and follow the path steeply uphill to reach the summit of the **Grosser Höllkogel**.

Trail to the Grosser Höllkogel

The **Grosser Höllkogel** (1862m) is the highest peak on the Höllengebirge, and the views are magnificent, in particular south across the vast wall of the Hohe Schott to Dachstein, and just to the left of the Hohe Schott, the sprawling plateau of the Totes Gebirge.

Descend to the Riederhütte trail and turn L along this, ascending gradually with views of the hut ahead, to reach **Riederhütte**, 20min from the junction below the Grosser Höllkogel.

Riederhütte (open late May–late October, food and accommodation) makes a wonderful spot for lunch, with a nice terrace and views of the Grosser Höllkogel. The present hut was built in 1977, replacing an older one destroyed by fire.

Follow the path leading E from Riederhütte, with views stretching out across the north edge of the Höllengebirge, to reach the junction with your outgoing route in 30min. Turn L here and follow your outgoing route back to the **Feuerkogel** upper cable car station (allow 1hr 30min).

WALK 13

*Offensee to Rinnerhütte and
Wildensee*

Start/finish	Offensee car park (Offensee parkplatz Ost)
Distance	14km
Ascent/descent	1145m
Grade	Medium
Time	6hr
Terrain	Rocky but well-marked trails, steep in places, some 4x4 tracks at the start
Maximum altitude	1580m
Maps	Alpenverein no. 15/1 Totes Gebirge West (1:25,000); Kompass no. 229 Salzkammergut Sheet 2 (1:50,000)
Refreshments	Rinnerhütte (tel +43 (0)664 2405 181 or +43 (0)680 5569 635)
Transport	Traunsee Taxi run a shuttle service between Ebensee and the car park on the east shore of Offensee (Parkplatz Ost) between 0700 and 2000 (Line 41, departing Ebensee railway station or Feurkogel lower cable car station, one-way fare €6, tel +43 (0)50 422 422). Call at least 1hr ahead to book, preferably earlier. Note that there is no mobile signal at Offensee, or most of the way up to Rinnerhütte either, so you need to arrange your pickup from Offensee before setting off from Ebensee.

This is a wonderful, exhilarating route on the north edge of the Totes Gebirge, starting on the shores of the idyllic Offensee and climbing to a lovely little hut, Rinnerhütte, and one of the most beautifully wild and remote-feeling lakes anywhere in Salzkammergut. It can be extended to include a climb on Rinnerkogel (2012m) or, with an overnight or two, turned into a traverse of the Totes Gebirge via Albert Appelhaus to link with Walk 22. The standard timing usually given for Offensee to Rinnerhütte is 2hr 30min, but I found it was closer to 3hr.

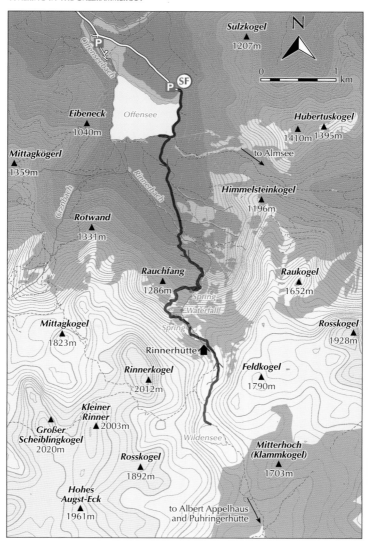

From the last car park at Offensee, follow the 4x4 road S alongside the shore of the lake, passing some tempting looking beaches, and a path on your L to Almsee. The lakeside trail soon bears R, but keep straight ahead on the 4x4 road, then bear R where the road forks, and R again where the 4x4 road splits a second time. Turn R on a path, cross a double footbridge over the streambed of the **Rinnerbach** (dry in August), to reach a bench and table 50min from the car park.

The path now leads uphill, steeply at times, passing a small shrine in a rock face after ascending a series of wooden steps, and a faint spring. A little under 2hr from the car park you arrive at a bench overlooking a **waterfall**, where the Rinnerbach tumbles down the cliff face in a long ribbon of spray. Continue past the bench, then up a flight of metal steps, after which the path bears R passing a dry streambed. Pass a good **spring** on your L at around 1180m (marked Rinnerboden-Brünndl on maps), then go up over scree slopes in a series of zigzags to a saddle, and downhill slightly beyond that to reach **Rinnerhütte**, 3hr from the Offensee car park.

Totes Gebirge, from the trail up to Rinnerhütte

Reflections in Offensee

Rinnerhütte (1473m, open mid-June–mid-September, and in fine weather weekends until mid-October, food and accommodation) sits in a lovely spot, and serves some wonderfully tasty *gulaschsuppe* and delicious homemade cakes. Built in 1934, and enlarged in the 1960s and 1970s, it makes an excellent base for exploring the north edge of the Totes Gebirge.

Follow the clear trail S from Rinnerhütte, ascending and passing the trail to Rinnerkogel (2012m, 1hr 45min to reach the top from here) to reach **Wildensee** in 30min.

At 1535m, **Wildensee** sits in a beautiful location below Rinnerkogel, quite some spot for a picnic – or a swim. The path straight ahead leads to Albert Appelhaus, and beyond this to Pühringerhütte and the Langangsee lakes (Walk 22).

This makes a nice spot to cool down after the walk.

Return to Offensee by the same route (allow 30min to Rinnerhütte, and another 2hr to reach Offensee). When you reach the lake, turn L along the lakeside trail for a little way. ◄ Then continue along the E shore to the **Offensee car park**.

WALK 14
Katrin (Seven Lakes View Trail)

Start	Katrin Seilbahn (upper station)
Finish	Katrin Seilbahn (lower station), Bad Ischl
Distance	7.5km
Ascent	340m
Descent	1265m
Grade	Easy–medium
Time	4hr 30min
Terrain	Good, clear mountain paths on the circuit, with one slightly exposed section secured with cables; steep forest paths on the descent to Bad Ischl
Maximum altitude	1638m (Hainzen)
Maps	Naturerlebniskarte Bad Ischl (1:45,000)
Refreshments	Katrin Berggasthof (www.katrin-berggasthof.at) and the more homely Katrin Almhütte (www.katrinalmhuette.com), both located beside the upper cable car station; Pizzeria Napoli opposite the lower seilbahn station is well placed for dinner at the end of your hike.
Transport	The Katrin cable car runs from the outskirts of Bad Ischl to just over 1400m (www.katrinseilbahn.com). Bus no. 150 to Bad Ischl, or train to Bad Ischl from Attnang-Puchheim or Obertraun.

Katrin is the name of the most visited peak of the Katergebirge, but is commonly used for the whole area. Lying at the centre of Salzkammergut, it makes for a fantastic viewpoint of the whole area, and the circular walk described here, known as the Sieben Seen Blick (Seven Lakes View), takes in views of many of the walks (peaks as well as lakes) described in this guide. Although there's a telecommunications tower on Katrin, it's behind you when you're admiring the view, and doesn't detract from the summit experience.

This walk makes use of the cable car for the ascent, but includes the walk back down to Bad Ischl on foot (for a shorter walk, you can obviously take the cable car down instead of walking, which would bring the distance and time down to 4km and 2hr 45min respectively). For a slightly longer walk, you could include a 1hr circular trail over the peak just east of the cable car station, called Feuerkogel (not to be confused with the better-known Feuerkogel on the Höllengebirge further north, see Walk 11).

From the town centre
To reach the cable car station from the centre of Bad Ischl (walking time 20min), follow the L bank of the Traun and walk through Sisipark, then along a path between the sports centre and a small stream (the Kaltenbach). Cross the stream on a footbridge, turn L along the asphalt road then along the main road to the cable car station.

From the upper cable car station, follow the 'Sieben Seen Blick' trail W, then take the R fork and follow the path uphill – passing a trail on your L which you'll follow later – to reach the large metal cross on **Katrin**, 30min from the upper cable car station.

While not the highest point on this walk, **Katrin** (1542m) has astonishingly good views over the Ischl Valley, including Wolfgangsee and Schafberg (Walk 7), Schwarzensee (just to the right of Schafberg), Mondsee (to the left of Schafberg), and Nussee nestled in the forest directly below Katrin.

The peak directly opposite you to the north is Zimnitz (also called Leonsberg), to which there's a good (but quite steep) route from Pfandl (with fabulous views of Schafberg from the summit). Beyond this can be seen the pale, high plateau of the Höllengebirge, including the Grosser Höllkogel (Walk 12). The prominent peak lying east-northeast with a 4x4 road climbing it in long zigzags is the Hoher Schott. The via ferrata (Katrin Klettersteig) route to Katrin comes up over the crag just north of the summit cross.

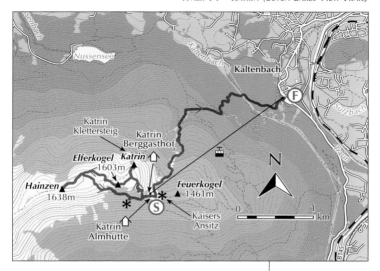

Retrace your steps from Katrin to the trail on your R and follow this W across **Elferkogel** (1603m), with good views of Hallstätter See to the S. Go straight ahead past a trail on your L, to an open area usually stacked with cairns (good views of Wolfgangsee), and then beyond this to reach the summit cross on **Hainzen**, just over 1hr from Katrin.

> **Hainzen** (1638m) has excellent views of Hallstätter See (Walk 23) and Dachstein (Walks 24–27). Those counting will have noticed that, so far, this 'Seven Lakes View' circuit has taken in views of only six lakes – not the seven promised by its title. That's because the seventh lake is actually Tachinger See, the northern portion of Waginger See, over the border in Germany – which you can see, just, on a very clear day, some 70km to the northwest. Apparently.

Retrace your steps from Hainzen to the previous trail junction and turn R, descending on a steep, rocky

View of the Hohe Schrott and Totes Gebirge from Katrin

A telescope is provided for enhanced views of the Hallstätter Glacier.

path. After 30min from Hainzen, go straight ahead past a trail on your L. Cross a slightly exposed section of trail secured by cables to reach a small wooden terrace overlooking Dachstein, 1hr from Hainzen. ◀

Continue past the **terrace** (viewpoint) for another 15min to reach the upper cable car station again.

Built in 1888, **Katrin Almhütte** (1393m, May–November open daily except Monday) is a cosy little hut with a nice terrace just below the cable car station, which makes a good spot for lunch. There's also the **Katrin Berggasthof** (1416m, open daily early April–mid November) beside the cable car station.

Regardless of whether you plan to take the cable car down or walk as described here, it's worth walking 2min to the small lookout point on the N side of the saddle between the upper cable car station and Feuerkogel, known as the **Kaisers Ansitz**.

To walk down from Katrin, take the trail N from the saddle between Katrin and Feuerkogel, which heads downhill following the course of the ski run. Keep straight across one, and then another 4x4 track, then bear L onto a forest path, steep in places. Cross another 4x4 track, then 1hr 30min from the cable car station turn R on a 4x4 track. ◀ Pass the water works, go under the cable car route, and keep straight ahead past a footbridge on your L. Just after a stream, take an unmarked path down on your L, to reach the lower cable car station 1hr 40min from the start of the descent.

Following the 4x4 track to the L would lead to Nussee.

WALK 15

Ewige Wand

Start	Bad Goisern railway station
Finish	Bad Goisern Jodschwefelbad railway station
Distance	7km
Ascent	500m
Descent	515m
Grade	Easy
Time	2hr 40min
Terrain	An easy route on 4x4 tracks and clear paths, with some sections on asphalt
Maximum altitude	814m (Ewige Wand)
Maps	Bad Goisern am Hallstätter See; Kompass no. 229 Salzkammergut Sheet 2 (1:50,000)
Refreshments	Rathlucken Hütte (www.rathlucka-huette.at/)
Transport	Train runs to Bad Goisern Jodschwefelbad and Bad Goisern from Bad Ischl or Obertraun (but note that not all trains stop at Bad Goisern Jodschwefelbad). Bus no. 542 runs between Gosau and Bad Ischl, stopping at Bad Goisern Mitte (on the B145) and Bad Goisern Jodschwefelbad station.

Ewige Wand (meaning 'the eternal wall') is a rock face stretching across the forested slopes of Predigstuhl, east of Bad Goisern, which can be traversed by a series of tunnels and galleries. There is a short but exposed via ferrata route across Ewige Wand (not included in this walk), and it's also popular as a mountain bike trail (using different ascent/descent routes from the ones described here). A series of wooden sculptures along the section of trail between Rathlucken Hütte and Ewige Wand, with accompanying legends written in German and English, makes this walk particularly fun for kids.

Ewige Wand lies on the route of the Salzkammergut Trophy, one of Austria's biggest mountain bike challenges which takes place in mid-July – so this route is not open to hikers at that time.

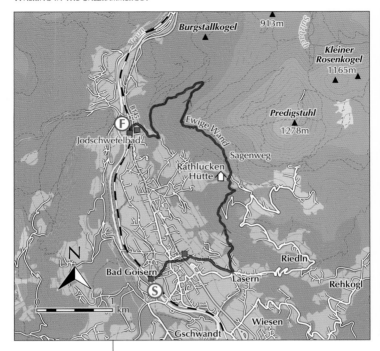

Walk NE from Bad Goisern railway station along Gottlieb-Oberhauser straße, crossing Untere Marktstraße and passing the Tourist Information Office (where it's worth picking up the free map) to reach the **main road** (B145) by the Bad Goisern Mitte bus stop. Cross the main road and turn R, then go L where the pedestrian pavement stops, following an asphalted alley marked as a mountain bike route. Keep straight ahead, then turn R onto an asphalt road leading gradually uphill past houses. Keep R where the road forks, then on reaching the settlement of **Lasern** turn L at the junction, just before a wooden shelter, and follow the asphalt road uphill.

After 10min from Lasern just before the point where the road forks, turn R and go up a steep concrete drive (unmarked) beside a house, then go L and follow the fence around the back of the house, going under the eaves at one point. Go uphill on a forest path, which levels off after a while and passes through a few clearings. Turn R on reaching a house, following an asphalt road then at a prominent wooden pole go L onto a path again, with views of the cliffs and tunnels of Ewige Wand ahead. The trail leads through forest again, becoming level with a stream below on the L. Go L over a wooden footbridge to reach **Rathlucken Hütte** (780m, closed Monday/Tuesday), 1hr from the railway station.

Continue N from the hut, on an asphalt road briefly then on a broad forest track, keeping straight ahead and passing a trail leading down on your L. Spread along this section of the route, called the **Sagenweg**, you'll pass a succession of wooden sculptures with accompanying texts retelling myths and fairytales. Bear L where the track forks (marked Ewige Wand and Radsteig Predstuhl), keeping level, to reach the galleries and tunnels of **Ewige Wand**.

'Wooden sculpture beside the Sagenweg

Ewige Wand

The tunnels and galleries on **Ewige Wand** were created in the mid-1950s by the local tourist office to develop hiking in the area and as an approach to Predigstuhl. There's also a short via ferrata route starting from one end of the tunnel, and ascending across the cliffs above the galleries.

At the end of the galleries, pass a viewpoint on your L, before continuing along the 4x4 track to a quarry. Turn L here and follow a track downhill, sometimes narrowing to a path, and marked bahnhof. Go L along a road then reach some houses, then take a path on your R (again marked bahnhof), continuing on a road again past more houses to reach the **main road** (B145) again. Cross the main road to arrive at **Bad Goisern Jodschwefelbad railway station**, 45min from Ewige Wand. The bus stop is in front of the station on the main road.

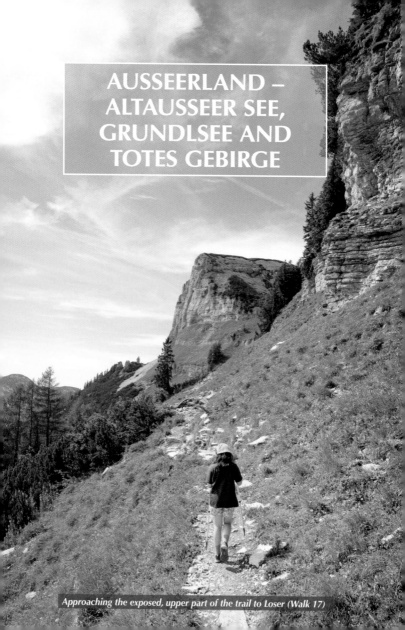

AUSSEERLAND – ALTAUSSEER SEE, GRUNDLSEE AND TOTES GEBIRGE

Approaching the exposed, upper part of the trail to Loser (Walk 17)

Ausseerland forms the southeast corner of Salzkammergut, and includes the spectacular, sprawling high karst plateau of the Totes Gebirge. The **Totes Gebirge** is one of the more remote parts of Salzkammergut, meaning that despite its name (translated as the 'Dead Mountains') it has quite well-preserved wildlife and plants – it forms part of the Northern Kalkalpen IBA (Important Bird Area) and contains several Natura2000 sites. Bordering the Totes Gebirge, the two main lakes are Altausseer See and **Grundlsee**, both of which have plenty of swimming spots, and there are several smaller lakes in the area including Toplitzsee, Kammerssee, Ödensee, and Vorderer and Hinterer Langangsee.

The hiking possibilities in Ausseerland are almost limitless – **Altausseer See** has one of the best lakeside walks in Salzkammergut (Walk 16); there are some beautiful hikes around Grundlsee, Toplitzsee and Kammersee (Walks 20 and 21); and Loser (Walk 17) and Trisselwand (Walk 18), on either side of Altaussee, command stupendous views of the Dachstein, the Totes Gebirge, and everything in between. Other rewarding day hikes in the area include Sandling (1717m), Zinken (1854m), Türkenkogel (1756m) and Kampl (1685m). Tauplitzalm, southeast of the routes described in this guide near Bad Mitterndorf, is one of Salzkammergut's best ski resorts. There are also some excellent

Ödensee in Ausseerland

mountain huts in the area, including Pühringerhütte (Walk 22), Rinnerhütte (Walk 13) and Albert Appelhaus (which can be used to link routes 22 and 13).

The salt mine at **Altaussee** (www. salzwelten.at), northwest of the town on the road to Sandling, is well worth visiting, and is particularly interesting for its later history. During World War 2 its tunnels were used as a storage depot by the Nazis, to store some of Hitler's vast accumulation of art treasures, on their way to the Führermuseum, his proposed new museum in Linz – including such masterpieces as the Ghent Altarpiece, and works by Albrecht Dürer, Rembrandt and Michelangelo. Towards the end of the war explosives were placed with the artworks, and instructions given that in the event of a German defeat, they were all to be destroyed. However, at their own initiative (and at the risk of certain execution if they were caught) local workers moved the explosives out into the woods and hid them there during the night.

During World War 2 Toplitzsee (Walks 20 and 21) was used by the Nazis as a testing area for explosives. There are also stories that some of the Nazis' looted gold was hidden in Toplitzsee, and people have been looking for it ever since – though as yet, no one has ever managed to find it. What have been found, however, are several cases of forged sterling banknotes (over £100 million), part of Hitler's Operation Bernhard which aimed to flood Britain with forged banknotes and induce a collapse of the UK economy, which were dumped in the lake by the SS at the end of World War 2, along with a printing press.

If you're in Ausseerland in mid-August, it's worth being in Altaussee for Berg im Flammen, a festival which takes place on a Saturday night, usually tying in with the weekend of Ascension Day. There's plenty of live music and dancing along the west shore of the lake, together with street food stalls and beer tents, and the evening culminates in burning torches being carried across the summits of Loser and Trisselwand, and by a surprisingly big firework display on the lake. You'll need to buy a ticket to enter the area between the parish church and the bridge over the Altausseer Traun, and you can expect all restaurants to be fully booked for the evening – but there's nothing to stop you having a picnic on one of the many beaches further around the lake, and watching the torch-lighting and fireworks from there, as many people do.

In the spring, Ausseerland is home to Austria's largest flower festival, the Narzissenfest or Daffodil Festival.

For the walks described in this guide, the most convenient base is Bad Aussee (Bad Mitterndorf is further away so less convenient for the walks in this guide, although it's connected to Bad Aussee by bus).

TRANSPORT

There are direct trains to Bad Aussee from Attnang-Puchheim via Ebensee, Bad Ischl, Bad Goisern and Obertraun, although not all services continue between Obertraun and Bad Aussee. Bus no. 952 runs between Bad Aussee and Bad Goisern; bus no. 950 runs between Bad Aussee and Bad Mitterndorf; bus no. 955 runs from Bad Aussee to Altaussee (Walks 16–19); bus no. 956 runs from Bad Aussee to Grundlsee and Gößl (Walks 20–22).

Ferries operate on Altausseer See (www.altausseeschifffahrt.at) and Grundlsee (www.schifffahrt-grundl see.at), and there are small traditional wooden boats on Toplitzsee (which you'll need to take to complete Walk 20, www.schifffahrt-grundlsee.at).

Taxi Zwetti (tel +43 (0)676 3622 605) and Taxi Gasperl (tel +43 (0)664 2000 902) are useful if you need to get back to Bad Aussee from Altaussee or Grundlsee if you miss the last bus – the fare from Bad Aussee to Altaussee is around €8. The two companies also run a shuttle service to Loser, departing from Bad Aussee at 0915, returning from Loser Alm at 1700 (€60 per van for up to 4 passengers, €13pp for 5 or more).

ACCOMMODATION

- **Bad Aussee** Haus Helpferer (Kramergasse 151, tel +43 (0)362 252608, holiday@helpferer.com; very little English spoken) is a small, simple but welcoming pension, a 10min walk south of the town centre.
- **Gößl** Hotel Jufa (Gößl 149, www. jufa.eu) is near Gößl on the south shore of Grundlsee.

TOURIST INFORMATION

There are tourist information offices in Bad Aussee (in the town centre, next to the Post Office) and in Altaussee (opposite the Kurhaus bus stop) https:// ausseerland.salzkammergut.at/.

WALK 16

Altausseer See circuit

Start/finish	Altaussee (parish church)
Distance	7.5km
Ascent/descent	335m
Grade	Easy
Time	2hr 30min
Terrain	A very easy walk on broad, level trails
Maximum altitude	830m
Maps	AV (Alpenverein) no. 15/1 Totes Gebirge West (1:25,000); Kompass no. 229 Salzkammergut Sheet 2 (1:50,000)
Refreshments	Jagdhaus Seeweisse (www.jagdhaus-seewiese.com) at the far (NE) end of the lake; Jausenstation Kahlseneck (www.kahlseneck.at); Strandcafe (www.strandcafe.at); restaurants in Altaussee
Transport	Bus no. 955 from Bad Aussee

One of the most beautiful and rewarding 'round the lake' walks in Salzkammergut, with good trails and awesome views of the northwest face of Trisselwand (Walk 18). It can be connected with a hike to Tressenstein (Walk 19), or even with Loser or Trisselwand (Walks 17 and 18 respectively) although with either of the latter two it would make for a long day. The walk is described in a clockwise direction here, but you could just as easily walk it in the opposite direction.

From the **parish church** in Altaussee, follow the asphalt road E, around to the L of the Hotel am See. The asphalt soon gives way to a 4x4 track, passing **Jausenstation Kahlseneck** (open Friday–Tuesday), then at the end of the track go through a gate by an old wooden mill (there are picnic benches and a good swimming spot just before this), and follow a path along the water's edge. ▶

After 40min from Altaussee, pass a trail on your R leading to a jetty where the ferry leaves for Altaussee. The

The 600m high W face of Trisselwand towers over the opposite shore of the lake.

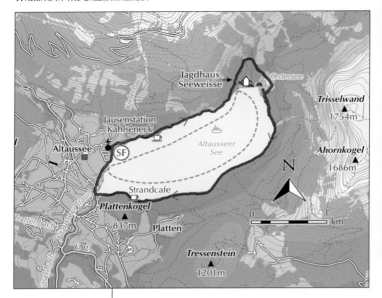

next trail on your R leads to Jagdhaus Seeweisse – take this if you plan to stop there for lunch, otherwise continue straight ahead along the slightly longer trail around the head of the lake (from further along where you can also reach the restaurant). Pass a trail to Albert Apfelhaus on your L, after which there are views over **Ostersee**, surrounded by marshy flats leading down to the shore of Altausseer See. After 25min from the turnoff to Jagdhaus Seeweisse, you pass the other trail leading to the restaurant, which crosses the outlet from Ostersee by a small footbridge.

Jagdhaus Seeweisse (open daily except Tues) sits in a beautiful location at the northeast corner of Altausseer See, flanked by the steep walls of Loser and Trisselwand. If you're here on Sundays or Wednesdays they have fresh char from the lake on the menu, but you need to order it and reserve a

table in advance. In 2015, the hut was used as a filming location for the James Bond film, *Spectre*.

Trisselwand reflected in Altausseer See

Continue along the S shore of the lake, which is dotted with plenty of beaches and secluded swimming spots. After 45min after the second trail to Jagdhaus Seeweisse, pass a 4x4 road on your L, which leads up to Platten and the trails to Trisselwand and Tressenstein (Walks 18 and 19 respectively), then pass the **Strandcafe** (a restaurant specialising in local freshwater fish, booking advised). Go onto the asphalt road, and turn R over the bridge across the **Altausseer Traun**, walking past the Seevilla Hotel and a small playground, and then the ferry jetty. Bear R along the asphalt lane which contours the lakeside, to arrive back at the **parish church** in Altaussee.

If you're in a hurry to catch the bus, you can take a shortcut – just after the playground near the ferry jetty, follow the track on your L which heads N over fields and past the football pitch to the car park by the Kurhaus bus stop.

WALK 17

Loser

Start/finish	Altaussee
Distance	15km
Ascent/descent	1290m
Grade	Difficult
Time	6hr 30min
Terrain	Good, clear paths up to Loserhütte, then a narrow trail across steep rocky slopes, exposed in places
Maximum altitude	1837m (Loser)
Maps	Alpenverein no. 15/1 Totes Gebirge West (1:25,000); Kompass no. 229 Salzkammergut Sheet 2 (1:50,000)
Refreshments	Loserhütte (www.willkommeninaltaussee.at)
Transport	Bus no. 955 to Altaussee

A steep but extremely beautiful hike to this iconic peak above Altaussee, straightforward as far as Loserhütte, but rocky and exposed after that. Loser (pronounced as the lo- in the English word 'lot', followed by the English word 'sir') stands at the southwest corner of the Totes Gebirge, its summit surrounded by cliffs on three sides and easy to spot from high peaks far across Salzkammergut. Loser Alm can also be reached by road, meaning that the hut can get quite busy, but the hike up from Altausser See is well worth doing. The route can be extended to include Hochanger and Augstsee.

From the Kurhaus bus stop in Altaussee, follow the main road E towards the lake then just before reaching the **parish church**, turn L up a side street (Altengasse, signposted to Loser). Go uphill and bear R, passing a marked 4x4 road on your L and a small wooden church on your R. Go straight ahead off the asphalt road onto a 4x4 track, then when the route splits into three take the trail on your L. ◀

The trail on the R marked 'zum' see leads down to the lake.

The trail becomes a nice, broad path which ascends gradually with views out over Altausseer See. After 1hr 30min from Altaussee, cross a 4x4 track, then 45min later

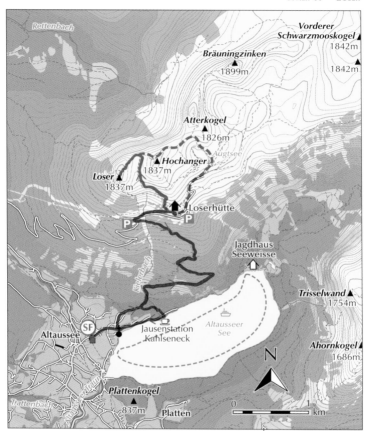

go under the chair lift. When you reach the car park turn R along the asphalt road then L up the ski run to reach **Loserhütte**, 2hr 45min from Altaussee.

> **Loserhütte** (1540m, open all year, food and accommodation) has a large terrace with a wonderful

113

view, although as it can be reached by road it tends to get extremely busy.

Retrace your steps along the ski run briefly then turn R and follow a path steeply uphill, turning L where this intersects with a trail coming in from your R. The two large rock barriers below are to prevent avalanches. The trail from this point is rocky and exposed in places, traversing NW across the steep slopes between Graskögerl and Loser, before entering a gently sloping grassy gully, and passing several dolines. At the far end of the gully, go L at the trail junction and ascend SW to reach the summit of **Loser**, 1h 15min from the hut. ◀

From the summit cross on Loser (1837m) there are stupendous views SW to Dachstein, and E over the Totes Gebirge.

Extension to Augtsee

From the junction NE of Loser, it's possible to extend this route by following the path E over Hochanger (1837m) passing the Loserfenster (a rock window with views to Schönberg) to **Augtsee**, a small lake below Atterkogel, and from there follow the road and the ski run back to Loserhütte. The route is a little exposed in places and would add an extra 1hr 45min to the walk. Or as easier

Loser viewed from Altaussee

alternative, follow the road from Loserhütte up to the Loser alm car park, from where it's an easy 10min walk to Augtsee.

Retrace your steps to Altaussee by the main route (allow 2hr 30min). If you want to stop beside Altausseer See on the way, turn L on the 4x4 road marked 'zum see' (about 15min above the town), which leads down to the lakeside trail (Walk 16) near Jausenstation Kahlseneck.

View back across the grassy area just before the last section to the summit of Loser

WALK 18
Trisselwand

Start/finish	Altaussee
Distance	16km
Ascent/descent	1245m
Grade	Medium–difficult
Time	8hr 45min
Terrain	A long route on steep, rocky mountain paths, exposed in places
Maximum altitude	1754m (Trisselwand)
Maps	Alpenverein no. 15/1 Totes Gebirge West (1:25,000); Kompass no. 229 Salzkammergut Sheet 2 (1:50,000)
Refreshments	Jagdhaus Seeweisse (www.jagdhaus-seewiese.com) at the far (NE) end of the lake (see Walk 16); Jausenstation Kahlseneck (www.kahlseneck.at); Strandcafe (www.strandcafe.at); restaurants in Altaussee.
Transport	Bus no. 955 to Altaussee

The hike to Trisselwand – the summit of which stands above a vast cliff on the east side of Altausseer See – makes for one of the most breathtakingly beautiful and rewarding walks anywhere in Salzkammergut. It's a longer but easier hike than Loser, and there's no road or hut so it's much more peaceful. The walk is described here from Altaussee, but you can also hike from Bad Aussee, joining the route up from Altaussee at Tressensattel (see Walk 19).

From the **parish church** in Altaussee, walk S along the asphalt lane running parallel to the shore of the lake, following Walk 16 in reverse – past the Seevilla Hotel, then L over the bridge and along the S shore of the lake.

Just after passing the **Strandcafe** (a restaurant specialising in local freshwater fish, bookings advised) turn R up a 4x4 road leading towards **Plattenkogel** and Obertressen, then after a couple of minutes go L onto a path marked Tressenstein. Turn R onto a 4x4 track, then

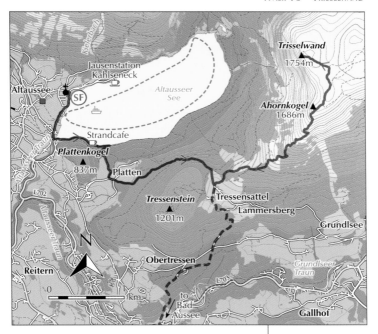

L onto a path alongside a house and L onto an asphalt road. Go straight ahead onto a 4x4 track through forest, passing a small cave in the bottom of a cliff before heading up steep steps, at the top of which is a small bench. After this the path levels out a bit, to reach a 4x4 road (leading on the R towards Tressenstein, Walk 19), a little over 1hr from the Strandcafe. Go straight across the 4x4 road and through a gate, then walk S across a field towards the houses of **Tressensattel**.

Turn L past Gasthaus Trisselwand (somewhat dishevelled on my visit), following a steep path knotted with tree roots. Cross a 4x4 road 40min from Tressensattel, continuing up a steep path which becomes increasingly rocky, and bear L up a series of steps aided by a handrail. ▶

As well as views back over Altausseer See, there are views of Grundlsee on the R as well, which you can admire from a lone bench on a corner of the trail.

At 2hr 30min from Tressensattel, pass a short trail on the L leading up to the summit cross on **Ahornkogel**, which is well worth the short detour either on the way up (or down) from Trisselwand – it's less than 5min up a steep path through dwarf mountain pine.

Ahornkogel (1686m) is a lovely spot, with fabulous views of Trisselwand as well as across Altausser See to Loser (Walk 17), and being slightly off the main trail it sees fewer hikers than Trisselwand itself.

Return to the main trail, and turn L across the level, grassy saddle between Ahornkogel and Trisselwand, pock-marked with dolines, and cross a steep area above the cliffs. Bear L where the trail splits (the path on the R goes to Albert Appelhaus), from where it's a final 20min uphill to the summit of **Trisselwand**.

The summit cross on **Trisselwand** (1754m) stands on a wide, grassy area directly above the 600m west face, and has unsurpassed views of the Totes Gebirge.

Return to Altaussee by the same route – allow 2hr 45min to Tressensattel, and a further 1hr 15min to Altaussee.

Ahornkogel, on the route to Trisselwand

If you want to descend from Tressensattel direct to Bad Aussee, see the description in Walk 19.

WALK 19

Tressenstein

Start/finish	Altaussee
Alt finish	Bad Aussee
Distance	10.5km
Ascent/descent	535m
Grade	Medium
Time	4hr 20min
Terrain	Easy forest trails and some 4x4 tracks
Maximum altitude	1201m (Tressenstein)
Maps	Alpenverein no. 15/1 Totes Gebirge West (1:25,000); Kompass no. 229 Salzkammergut Sheet 2 (1:50,000)
Refreshments	Strandcafe (www.strandcafe.at); Altaussee
Transport	Bus no. 955 to Altaussee, or train to Bad Aussee

Much lower and easier than its immediate neighbour Trisselwand, Tressenstein nevertheless has very good views from its summit – in part due to the presence of a tall wooden viewing tower there. Tressenstein lies roughly midway between Bad Aussee and Altaussee, and there are hiking trails from both towns up to Tressensattel (though on balance, the route from Altaussee is nicer), making it a convenient through route between them.

From the **parish church** in Altaussee, walk S along the asphalt lane running parallel to the shore of the lake, following Walk 16 in reverse – past the Seevilla Hotel, then L over the bridge and along the S shore of the lake.

Just after passing the **Strandcafe** (a restaurant specialising in local freshwater fish, bookings advised) turn R up a 4x4 road leading towards Plattenkogel and Obertressen, then after a couple of minutes go L onto a path marked Tressenstein. Turn R onto a 4x4 track, then L onto a path alongside a house and L onto an asphalt road. Go straight ahead onto a 4x4 track through forest, passing a small cave in the bottom of a cliff before heading

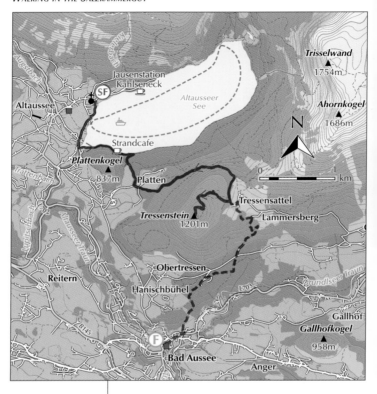

It's 54 steps up to the top of the tower on Tressenstein, with views across Altaussee and Grundlsee.

up steep steps, at the top of which is a small bench. After this the path levels out a bit to reach a 4x4 road, a little over 1hr from the Strandcafe. Turn R along the road (the gate straight ahead leads across a field to the houses of **Tressensattel** and the trail to Trisselwand, Walk 18), then a marked path on the R and go R where the trail forks. A final, steep section of path zigzags up to the base of the tower on **Tressenstein**, 40min from Tressensattel. ◄

Descend to Altaussee by the same route (allow 1hr 45min).

Descent to Bad Aussee

Alternatively, you can descend to Bad Aussee from Tressensattel in 1hr 30min. When you reach the 4x4 road on Tressensattel, turn R instead of L, and follow the road around to the L into the houses of **Tressensattel**. Turn R (S) onto a road which becomes a slightly overgrown track leading downhill through the trees. Bear L to emerge into a clearing, passing alongside the outhouses of a farmstead, then turn R down a grassy track, which becomes an asphalt road on reaching some houses. Go straight ahead across another road, downhill on a 4x4 track through forest, and bear R. Go past the houses of **Hanischbühel** on a 4x4 track, then an asphalt path. Go L down a path into Bad Aussee, crossing the bridge over the **Grundlseer Traun**, then turn R and follow Hauptstraße to the Bad Aussee Postant bus stop in the centre of town.

Tressenstein from Altausseer See

WALK 20

Grundlsee, Toplitzsee and Kammersee

Start	Grundlsee (Archkogl)
Finish	Gößl ladner bus stop (Murbodenhüttl)
Distance	15.5km
Ascent	630m
Descent	630m
Grade	Medium
Time	6hr
Terrain	Easy walking on a mixture of lakeside and forest trails, 4x4 tracks and some asphalt roads
Maximum altitude	885m (Zimnitzbach waterfall)
Maps	Alpenverein no. 15/1 Totes Gebirge West (1:25,000); Kompass no. 229 Salzkammergut Sheet 2 (1:50,000)
Refreshments	Fischerhütte (www.toplitzsee.at); Murbodenhüttl (www.murbodenhuettl.com); Rostiger Anker (www.rostiga-anker.at) and others in Gößl
Transport	Bus no. 956 from Bad Aussee. The short trail from Toplitzsee to Kammersee is only accessible by boat – boats leave Fischerhütte every half an hour or so, with the return journey lasting about 1hr which includes waiting time while passengers hike the short trail to Kammersee.

A walk around the south shore of Grundlsee, to the lovely Toplitzsee and Kammersee, the lakes which form the eponymous view in the hike to Drei Seen Blick (Walk 21). Kammersee is only accessible by boat, so a boat trip across Toplitzsee in a traditional wooden *plätten* is included in this itinerary. (The boat trip is included in the timing, but not in the distance figure above; you'll also need to allow a bit of waiting time for the next boat departure.) The walk can conveniently be cut short in Gößl, but it's worth continuing around to the northeast corner of the lake as described here to see the impressive Zimitzbach waterfall.

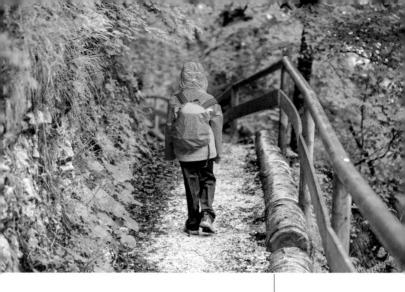

From the bridge over the Grundlseer Traun at the W outlet of Grundlsee, follow the road S through Archkogl (also written Archkogel). After turning E, bear R and uphill through woodland, then turn L along an asphalt road. After 30min from the bridge, the asphalt road peters out and you continue along a 4x4 track which soon becomes a path above the S shore of Grundlsee, below the steep N slopes of Ressen. Go onto an asphalt road again, then L onto a forest path, then on an asphalt road through the houses of **Wienern**, to reach **Hotel Jufa** on your L, 2hr from Archkogl. Follow the asphalt road around the E end of Grundlsee, crossing the bridge over the **Stimitzbach**.

On the trail above the south shore of Grundlsee

Just before the bridge over the **Toplitzbach**, on the edge of **Gößl**, turn R onto a 4x4 road signposted to Toplitzsee and Drei Seen Blick (Walk 21). Bear L where the road forks, and go straight ahead uphill passing a footbridge on your L. Arriving on the shore of **Toplitzsee**, turn L over the footbridge with its wooden sluice gate to arrive at **Fischerhütte** (closed Wednesdays), a popular restaurant specialising in local freshwater fish, with a large terrace beside the lake, 30min from Gößl.

Toplitzsee (718m) is a narrow, elongated lake, stretching for around 2km below steep-sided slopes. It's comparatively deep – 103m – and is fed only by two waterfalls, which flow down from the high peaks of the Totes Gebirge on its north side, and by an underground channel from neighbouring Kammersee. Toplitzsee is a meromictic lake, that is, its surface and deepwater layers are only partially mixed, and the deepwater layer – in the case of Toplitzsee, water below 20m – has no oxygen and a much higher salinity.

There are rumours that hidden somewhere in the depths of Toplitzee is a fortune in Nazi gold,

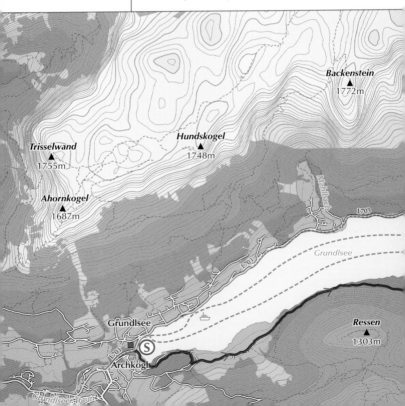

sunk there at the end of World War 2 (see section introduction). These stories have spawned a spree of treasure hunting expeditions over the years, but the depth of the lake and the fact that the bottom is buried beneath a lethal mass of submerged logs, has meant that so far no one has found this legendary treasure, if indeed it does exist – though some have died trying.

Plätten – traditional, flat-bottomed wooden boats – take passengers to the far end of Toplitzsee, with a guided commentary (in German, but the crew will be happy to answer questions in English) about the lake and local history. Tickets cost

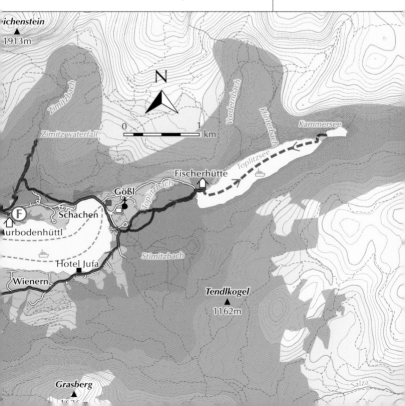

Traditional flat-bottomed wooden boats (Plätten) moored on Toplitzsee

€10, which covers the return journey including around 20min waiting time for passengers to visit Kammersee on foot (www.schifffahrt-grundlsee.at).

Take the boat to the far end of Toplitzsee, then follow the short path to arrive at **Kammersee** in under 5min.

Unlike Toplitzsee, the diminutive **Kammersee** is just 7m deep. Hemmed in by boulders, cliffs and forest (if you look up at the cliffs almost due east you might be able to spot the lookout point, Drei Seen Blick, the destination of Walk 21), its only outflow being through an underground channel into Toplitzsee. As you walk between Toplitzsee and Kammersee, note the narrow channel cut through the rock near the trail. This was hacked out in the 18th century to allow logs – for which there was huge demand from the salt works at Bad Aussee – to be transported between the two lakes.

Walk back to Toplitzsee and take the boat back to Fischerhütte, then retrace your steps towards Grundlsee, turning R onto a path which descends and follows the Toplitzbach before crossing a footbridge to rejoin your outward route, just before the main road and Grundlsee. Turn R along the main road into **Gößl**.

You can if you want finish the walk here in Gößl. Ferries depart from a jetty on the N side of the village near the roundabout, and bus no. 956 to Bad Aussee departs from the shelter just N of the roundabout. If you're looking for somewhere to eat in Gößl, Rostiga Anker has a large terrace near the lake.

> The main settlement of **Gößl** is set back from Grundlsee, below a massive cliff, the Gößlerwand. The small church, built and owned by 14 local families, was completed in 1821. There's also a sporadic music and art festival in Gößl (www.sprudel sprudel-musik.com).

Follow the main road around the N shore of Grundlsee then after 10min take a path on your R, which leads up through forest. Go straight ahead over a 4x4 road, and past the water works, following the occasional signpost marked 'wasserfall'. Bear R and cross the footbridge over the powerful **Zimitzbach**, with an old mill building on your L, then cross a smaller bridge and ascend past a braided stream. Turn R along a good track below a rock face, and follow this uphill for 20min to reach a narrow path on your R, leading to a viewing platform in front of the **waterfall**.

Retrace your steps but keep straight ahead where your outward route comes in from the L. The trail continues downhill gradually to join a 4x4 road, still on the R bank of the Zimitzbach, which leads to the main road running along the north shore of Grundlsee, 40min from the waterfall. Turn L on the main road, crossing the bridge over the Zimitzbach, to reach the Gößl ladner bus stop (bus no. 956 to Bad Aussee) and the well-placed **Murbodenhüttl** (open all year).

WALK 21
Drei Seen Blick

Start/finish	Gößl
Distance	12.5km
Ascent/descent	725m
Grade	Medium
Time	4hr 30min
Terrain	Easy walking on 4x4 tracks and forest trails, with only one very short, mildly exposed section
Maximum altitude	1204m (Drei Seen Blick)
Maps	AV (Alpenverein) no. 15/1 Totes Gebirge West (1:25,000) & AV (Alpenverein) no. 15/2 Totes Gebirge Mitte (1:25,000); Kompass no. 229 Salzkammergut Sheet 2 (1:50,000)
Refreshments	Gößl
Transport	Bus no. 956 to Gößl

A hike to the well-known Drei Seen Blick or 'Three Lakes View', which overlooks Kammersee, Toplitzsee and Grundlsee.

From the bus stop or ferry landing in Gößl, follow the main road S then just after crossing the bridge over the **Toplitzbach**, turn L on a 4x4 road signposted Toplitzsee and Drei Seen Blick. Bear R where the road forks (not signposted) then keep straight ahead uphill, passing a trail on your R, then a small climbing area on your L. Pass a trail to Toplitzsee on your L, and cross the Geotrail which loops through this area.

After 30min from Gößl, go R on a path, crossing a plank bridge and heading uphill to gain a broad forest trail, which ascends gradually with glimpses of **Toplitzsee** below. Bear L where the trail forks (unmarked), to reach a 4x4 road 1hr 30min from Gößl.

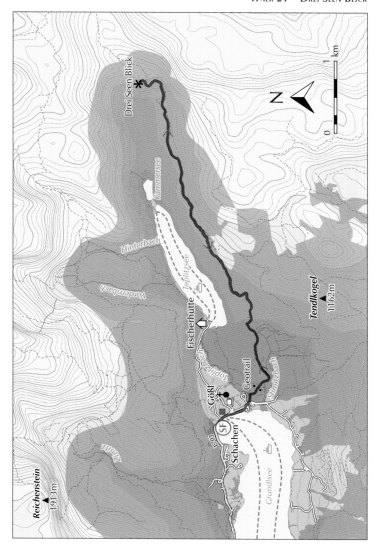

Turn L and follow the 4x4 road for 30min before taking a marked path on your R, then after a further 25min turn L on a level path with a pictogram signpost. A short, slightly exposed section secured with cables leads up to **Drei Seen Blick**, where a couple of simple benches look out across Kammersee, Toplitzsee and Grundlsee, from above a cliff. ◄

See Walk 20 for information on Toplitzsee and Kammersee.

Return to Gößl by the same route (allow 2hr).

3 Seen Blick: Kammersee, Toplitzsee and Grundlsee

WALK 22

Vorderer and Hinterer Lahngangsee
and Pühringerhütte

Start/finish	Gößl
Distance	20km
Ascent/descent	1240m
Grade	Medium–difficult
Time	7hr
Terrain	Good trails through forest then over open tops; slightly exposed in places and secured with cables
Maximum altitude	1638m (Pühringerhütte)
Maps	AV (Alpenverein) no. 15/1 Totes Gebirge West (1:25,000) & AV (Alpenverein) no. 15/2 Totes Gebirge Mitte (1:25,000); Kompass no. 229 Salzkammergut Sheet 2 (1:50,000)
Refreshments	Pühringerhütte (www.alpenverein.at/puehringerhuette/)
Transport	Bus no. 956 from Bad Aussee

This is an outstandingly beautiful walk to a series of wonderfully remote-feeling lakes: Vorderer and Hinterer Lahngangsee, as well as Elmsee, high up in the Totes Gebirge. The walk can be extended with an overnight at Pühringerhütte to include nearby peaks, and by continuing via Wildensee to Rinnerhütte it can be linked to Walk 13, creating a superb crossing of the Totes Gebirge.

From the bus stop in Gößl walk S to the roundabout and turn L, and follow the road NE past a small, lone **church**. Go L again then R over the stream, then just before an old house with garden gnomes along the windowsill turn L along a path marked Pühringerhütte.

The path zigzags up through forest, then goes diagonally across a 4x4 road. Turn R at the T-junction, then where the trail splits go R (not L to Zimitzalm). Go straight ahead across another 4x4 track, after which the trail

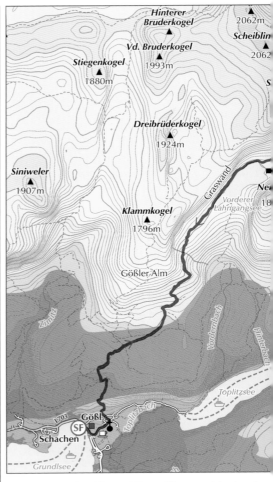

becomes more level for a while, and keep straight ahead past a trail on the L to Gößler Alm in a clearing. The path steepens again and crosses a steep escarpment, slightly exposed and secured with cables. Go over a saddle and

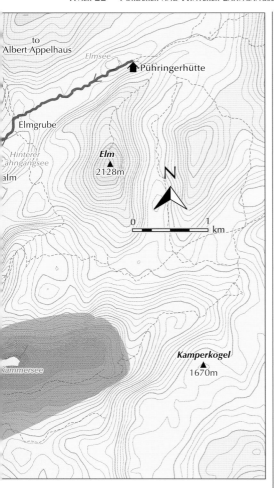

across steep, open slopes below the **Graswand**, then along a winding path to reach the shore of the first lake, **Vorderer Lahngangsee**, 2hr from Gößl.

Vorderer Lahngangsee in low cloud

Vorderer Lahngangsee is a wonderful spot, equally beautiful whether bathed in sunshine or, as on my first visit, wreathed in clouds, the view north-east along the lake framed by the Graswand and Neustein. A few wooden huts of Lahngangalm are scattered along the southeast shore.

Follow the narrow, rocky path along the NW shore of the lake, the view ahead of you framed by the Graswand (L) and the Neustein (R). You might find a thick tongue of snow to cross at the far end of the lake. Beyond Vorderer Lahngangsee the path ascends again, keeping NE and crossing the hillside higher above the second lake, **Hinterer Lahngangsee**, to reach the small cluster of wooden cottages at **Elmgrube**, surrounded by larch trees. At the trail junction bear R. ◀ Continue NE, passing two sinkhole shafts (the Kleines and Grosses Windloch) with cold air flowing up out of them, to reach to Elmsee and **Pühringerhütte**, 1hr 30min from the W end of Vorderer Lahngangsee.

The trail on the L goes to Albert Appelhaus.

Pühringerhütte (1 June–early October, food and accommodation) makes a great base for exploring this part of the Totes Gebirge, for those who want to stay for one or two nights. There are several peaks to climb nearby, including Elm (2128m, 1hr 30min), Hochkogel (2094m, 1h) and an exposed route to Rotgschirr (2261m, 3hr 30min.)

Descend to Gößl by the same route (allow 3hr 30min).

DACHSTEIN, HALLSTÄTTER SEE AND GOSAUSEE

On the trail to Taubenkogel

The **Dachstein** is a massive limestone plateau measuring roughly 20km by 30km, bordered by Hallstätter See to the north and rising on its southern edge to the Hoher Dachstein, at 2996m the roof of both Upper Austria and Styria, and the only mountain in either state with glaciers, which are the northernmost and easternmost in the Alps. Formed from a 1.5km thick wedge of Triassic reef limestone, it falls in an almost sheer drop on its southern edge, while its sprawling, heavily karstified eastern half is known simply as Am Stein. It's a wonderful area for hiking (Walks 24–27), among breathtaking scenery.

The pretty lakeside town of **Hallstatt** was the centre of a thriving salt mining industry from well before the Iron Age, and the whole story of Salzkammergut, both its wealth and its name, stem from here. The salt mines here can be visited (www.salzwelten.at/en/), with a funicular whisking people up to the visitor centre from Hallstatt, and the views out over the lake from beside the nearby Rudolfsturm are quite spectacular. Dachstein and Hallstatt together form a UNESCO World Heritage Site, and are enormously popular as a one- or two-day trip from Salzburg – but the crowds soon disappear once you move beyond the cable car routes and roads.

The Gosautal stretches southwest from **Hallstätter See**, curving south to the extraordinarily beautiful Gosausee lakes (Walk 28), set below the saw-tooth spine of the Gosaukamm. Hidden in the hills to the north of the Gosausee lakes is an area of rare blanket bog (Löckermoos, Walk 29), while crossing to the south of the Gosaukamm (Walk 30) opens up whole new panoramas on the southern flanks of the Dachstein.

Other hikes around the edge of the Dachstein massif include Plassen (1953m), the Hoher Sarstein (1975m), Hoch Kalmberg (1833m) and Gamsfeld (2027m), and there are plenty of short easy trails from the East Coast Trail on Hallstätter See (Walk 23) and the route through the Koppental, to the trail to the Waldbachstrub through the Echerntal (the wildly romantic scenery which has attracted artists and poets over the centuries, and the first part of which forms the start of Walk 24), and longer trips like the Dachstein Rundweg (of which Walk 30 forms one part). There are also some seriously impressive caves worth visiting (https://dachstein-salzkammergut.com/en/summer/below-ground/), even though they do sometimes come with a smidgen of kitsch (they are particularly handy when hiking plans are scuppered by the weather).

TRANSPORT

There are direct trains between Bad Ischl (and stations further north) and Bad Aussee, calling at Bad Goisern, Obersee, Hallstatt, Obertraun and Koppenbrüllerhöhle.

Bus no. 543 runs from Obertraun railway station to the lower Krippenstein cable car station – the service isn't very frequent; however, it's only a 35min walk: go out of the railway station, turn right along the main road passing the supermarket and Gasthof Höllwirt, then right over the railway line and alongside fields, cross the bridge over the River Traun, turn left past Gasthof Dachsteinhof and follow an asphalt lane uphill, then a 4x4 track through the mountain bike area to arrive in front of the cable car station.

The Dachstein-Krippenstein Seilbahn (https://dachstein-salz kammergut.com/en/) runs between Obertraun, Krippenstein and Gjaidalm. It's worth mentioning that on its first two sections, the Dachstein Krippenstein cable car can get absolutely packed. If it's busy (and it probably will be) try to be at or near the front of the queue at the ticket barriers, even if it means waiting for the next car – that way you'll at least be by a window with a view, rather than squashed in the middle or by the door like a sardine, which can be a bit of a miserable end to a spectacular hiking experience (once you're through the ticket barriers, you will have to get in that particular car).

To get to Hallstatt (Walk 24): if you're arriving by train from further north or from Bad Aussee, get off at Hallstatt railway station (which is on the eastern shore of the lake, before Obertraun, not in Hallstatt itself) and

take the ferry over to Hallstatt (time-tables at www.hallstattschifffahrt.at) – the ferries are timed to meet the trains, so this will be faster than taking a bus from Obertraun to Hallstatt; otherwise, if you're already in Obertraun, take bus no. 543 from Obertraun railway station to Hallstatt Lahn (timetables at www.postbus.at).

To get to Gosausee (Walks 28–30): Bus no. 542 runs from Bad Ischl to Gasthof Gosausee via Bad Goisern (connecting with bus no. 952 to Bad Aussee) and Gosaumühle (connecting with bus no. 543 to Hallstatt and Obertraun), timetables at www. postbus.at

---

ACCOMMODATION

- **Obertraun** (Walks 23–24): Obertraun Haus Alpenrose (Obertraun 175, www.hausalpen rose.at/en-gb is close to the railway station.
- **Hallstatt** (Walk 24): Gasthof Grüner Anger (Lahn 10, http:// anger.hallstatt.net) lies at the start of Walk 24.
- **Dachstein** (Walks 24–27): Gjaidalm (www.gjaid.at); Wiesberghaus (www.wies berghaus.at); Simonyhütte (www. simonyhuette.com).
- **Gosausee** (Walks 28–30): Gasthof Gosausee (Gosausee, www. gasthof-gosausee.at): small, friendly and good value guest-house with a nice restaurant; guestrooms at the front overlook

Großer Donnerkogel and Gosaukamm above Vorderer Gosausee (Walks 28, 29 and 30)

the lake and have a perfect view of the Hohe Dachstein; cash only. There are also hotels and guesthouses in Hallstatt and Obertraun.

PRACTICAL INFORMATION

Apart from a small snack and souvenir kiosk, there are no shops at the end of the road, near Gasthof Gosausee – the nearest shops (and the nearest ATM) are back in Gosau.

TOURIST INFORMATION

- Offices in Obetraun (Obertraun 180) and Hallstatt (Seestraße 99) https://dachstein.salzkammergut. at/en.

WALK 23

Hallstätter See East Shore Trail

Start	Obersee (railway station)
Finish	Obertraun (railway station)
Distance	5km
Ascent	95m
Descent	95m
Grade	Easy
Time	2hr
Terrain	Easy tracks and paths
Maximum altitude	540m
Maps	Kompass no. 229 Salzkammergut Sheet 2 (1:50,000)
Refreshments	Obertraun; Schutzhütte Koppental (www.koppental.at/); Bad Aussee
Transport	Train to Obersee/Obertraun (note that not all trains stop at Obersee, check timetables at www.oebb.at/)

The East Bank Trail is a very easy, well-known path along the shore of Hallstätter See between the railway stations at Obersee and Obertraun, with wonderful views of Plassen, the Dachstein peaks and the picture-perfect town of Hallstatt ahead. It can be walked in either direction, but the views are best walking south.

For a longer walk you can combine this with a visit visit to the Koppenbrüllerhöhle, or continue along the Koppental Trail, which runs through the surprisingly wild valley of the River Traun, between Obertraun and Bad Aussee (allow an additional 4hr for the Koppental Trail, plus at least an extra hour for a detour and visit to the Koppenbrüllerhöhle.

From the railway station in Obersee, walk S alongside Hallstätter See, parallel to the railway line, with views of the little town of Hallstatt ahead on the opposite shore, with the entrance to the Echerntal beyond (Walk 24). Schneidkogel rises steeply above Hallstatt, with Plassen visible behind it, and you can see the funicular leading

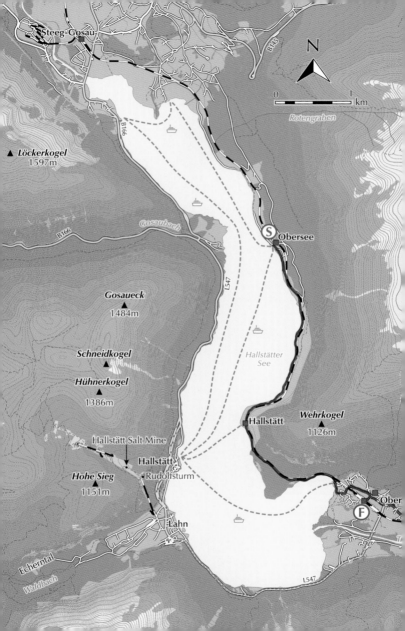

up to the **Rudolfsturm** near the entrance to the salt mines. Go past small beaches then along a metal walkway above the water, before turning inland and uphill, to arrive on the platform of Hallstatt railway station.

Turn R along the platform, keeping straight ahead past an asphalt path on the R which leads down to the ferry jetty. Follow a track parallel to the railway line, passing behind the raised headland which protrudes at this corner of Hallstätter See, which leads you to a small dock and footbridge on the edge of Obertraun. Go L under the railway line, then R along the main road and R again to reach **Obertraun railway station**.

Extension to Koppenbrüllerhöhle through the Koppental

It's a 1hr walk from Obertraun to Koppenbrüllerhöhle station, alongside the River Traun, then beside the railway line, then a further 1km along the left bank of the Traun to **Koppenbrüllerhöhle**.

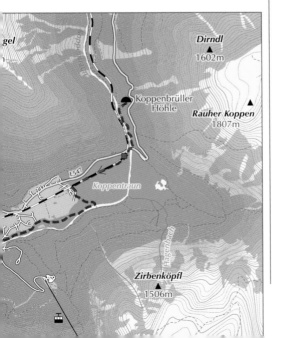

View across Hallstätter See

The cave, **Koppenbrüllerhöhle**, is well worth visiting (https://dachstein-salzkammergut.com/en/summer/below-ground/, with tours of the cave lasting 50min). The route north from the cave down to the Traun was closed due to erosion in 2019.

WALK 24

Hallstatt to Weisberghaus and
Gjaidalm via Echerntal

Start	Hallstatt Lahn
Finish	Gjaidalm (upper Krippenstein cable car station)
Distance	15km
Ascent	1840m
Descent	570m
Grade	Medium
Time	7hr 15min
Terrain	Good, clear paths throughout, with an extended section on asphalt road along the Echerntal
Maximum altitude	1884m (Wiesberghaus)
Maps	AV (Alpenverein) no. 14 Dachstein (1:25,000); Kompass no. 229 Salzkammergut Sheet 2 (1:50,000)
Refreshments	Wiesberghaus (www.wiesberghaus.at); Gjaidalm (www.gjaid.at)
Transport	The Dachstein-Krippenstein Seilbahn (https://dachstein-salzkammergut.com/en/) runs between Obertraun, Krippenstein and Gjaidalm (at the end of this walk); bus no. 543 runs between Obertraun railway station and Hallstätt, stopping at the lower Krippenstein cable car station (timetables at www.postbus.at); or from Hallstatt railway station take the ferry over to Hallstatt (timetables at www.hallstattschifffahrt.at) – this will be faster than continuing by train to Obertraun then taking a bus to Hallstatt.

A magnificent walk, starting in Hallstatt and finishing at the upper station of the Dachstein-Krippenstein Seilbahn near Gjaidalm, where you can take the cable car down to Obertraun. The route follows the beautiful Echerntal initially, before climbing steadily up to the Wiesberghaus which is set amongst wonderful mountain scenery, then onward along the Dachstein Nature Trail to Gjaidalm.

Although not technically difficult, it's a fairly long hike, with a considerable amount of ascent. However, the route can conveniently be spread over two days if preferred, with an overnight stay at Wiesberghaus or Gjaidalm. The section of the route between Wiesberghaus and Gjaidalm could then be combined with the trail to Simonyhütte (Walk 25) and/or the Heilbronner Trail (Walk 27), before taking the cable car from Krippenstein down to Obertraun.

From the bus stop in Hallstatt Lahn, follow the street S along the waterfront (Seelande), crossing the **Waldbach**, then turn right along Hubneranerweg. Turn L along the main road then immediately right onto an asphalt road, the Malerweg, passing **Gasthof Grüner Anger** on your right. (If you've arrived by ferry, walk S through the pretty old town then turn R along Echerntalweg, passing the Salzbergbahn on your R and crossing the Waldbach, to reach the Malerweg.)

Follow the asphalt road up the **Echerntal**, parallel to the Waldbach, then turn left onto a gravel path opposite a water trough. ◄ The path meanders alongside a stream, before rejoining the road. Pass a small shelter and the continuation of the Waldbachstub **waterfall trail** on your R, followed by a **memorial** on your left.

The memorial is to the great Austrian geographer **Friedrich Simony** (1830–96), who was co-founder of the Austrian Alpine Club and a pioneer in the exploration of the Dachstein massif.

Keep straight ahead on the road, signposted Wiesberghaus and Simonyhütte. As the road climbs gradually upwards, the view begins to open out. ◄ Where the road forks, keep left on the asphalt road, not the 4x4 heading down on your right. Pass the lower station of the supply cable running up to Wiesberghaus and follow the road through a short tunnel, then where the asphalt road swings right over a bridge, turn left onto a 4x4 road beside a rushing stretch of the Waldbach as it churns along its narrow, rocky streambed.

The valley was a favourite spot with Romantic poets and painters in the 19th century, including Ferdinand Georg Waldmüller and Rudolf von Alt.

There's a magnificent view of the Waldbachstrub and other waterfalls which tumble down above the forest at the head of the valley.

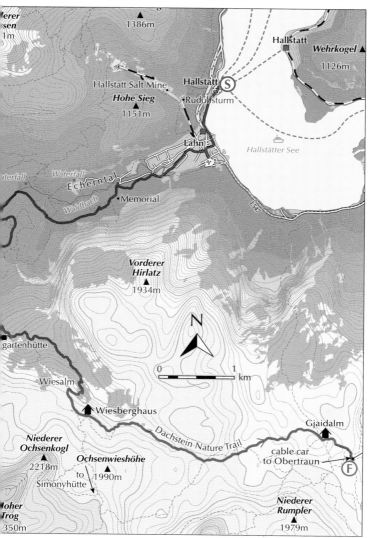

After 1hr 30min from Lahn, turn left onto a clearly marked path signposted to Wiesberghaus. The path zigzags steadily uphill, passing **Tiergartenhütte** (private) on the right at around 1460m. Continue ascending to reach the near edge of the level pasture at **Wiesalm**, where you bear right and go under the supply cable, before turning left and following the ridge up to **Wiesberghaus**, 4hr 30min from Lahn.

Wiesberghaus (open mid-May–late October, food and accommodation) sits at an altitude of 1884m, its location commanding sweeping views of the jagged spine of Plassen to the north, and the Niederer Ochsenkogel and other peaks to the southwest. It's one of the nicest huts in the Dachstein area and in Salzkammergut as a whole, and if you're planning to split the route over two days, Wiesberghaus is definitely the best choice for accommodation and food, and has a much more remote feeling than Gjaidalm and Krippenstein Lodge, both of which are accessible by 4x4 road or cable car.

*Waterfalls at the head
of the Echerntal*

To continue to Gjaidalm, walk SE from Wiesberghaus, contouring the side of the small knoll in front of the hut. The route from Wiesberghaus to Gjaidalm follows part of the clearly marked **Dachstein Nature Trail**, which stretches between Gjaidalm and Simonyhütte (Walk 25). About 1hr from Wiesberghaus, after winding through a landscape of rocky dells studded with juniper, pass a trail on your R (path no. 650) leading to Simonyhütte, from the junction of which there are phenomenal views of the Hoher Dachstein. Some 30min later bear left where the trail forks and descend to reach **Gjaidalm**, 2hr from Wiesberghaus, which sits beyond a grassy area alongside a 4x4 road.

On the trail between Wiesberghaus and Gjaidalm after October snowfall

> **Gjaidalm** (1738m, open all year, food and accommodation) is a large hut set above a lush meadow, at the start of a multitude of routes on Dachstein. Being so close to the cable car it gets quite busy in the summer, but it's still a beautiful spot, with excellent buffet dinners.

If you're not staying at Gjaidalm, continue along the 4x4 road in front of the hut, with one last short, but rather cruel, climb uphill, to reach the Gjaidalm station of the **Dachstein-Krippenstein Seilbahn**, 15min from Gjaidalm. Take the cable car to Krippenstein and then down to Obertraun.

WALK 25
Dachstein Nature Trail

Start/finish	Gjaidalm
Distance	13.5km
Ascent/descent	800m
Grade	Medium
Time	6hr
Terrain	Excellent mountain paths through varied terrain, slightly exposed in places, with some sections secured with cables
Maximum altitude	2203m (Simonyhütte)
Maps	AV (Alpenverein) no. 14 Dachstein (1:25,000); Kompass no. 229 Salzkammergut Sheet 2 (1:50,000)
Refreshments	Gjaidalm (www.gjaid.at/); Wiesberghaus (www.wiesberghaus.at/); Simonyhütte (www.simonyhuette.com)
Transport	Dachstein Seilbahn https://dachstein-salzkammergut.com/en/

The most beautiful walk on Dachstein is not, as most tourist office websites would have you believe, the Heilbronner Trail (Walk 27), but this one, known as the Dachstein Nature Trail – a magnificent route between Gjaidalm, Wiesberghaus and Simonyhütte, with fabulous views of the high Dachstein peaks and the Hallstätter glacier. The route is described here from Gjaidalm but can equally well be walked from the more remote-feeling Wiesberghaus.

Although this walk could be done as a day trip from Obertraun or Hallstätt, taking an early morning cable car up to Gjaidalm, it would make it an unnecessarily long and expensive day, and it's far more enjoyable as a day trip from Gjaidalm or Wiesberghaus, with one or two overnights there, especially in combination with Walk 24 as a walk-in from Hallstatt, and Walk 27 (in reverse).

Follow the path W from in front of Gjaidalm, then turn L on path no. 650 which goes along the edge of a wet

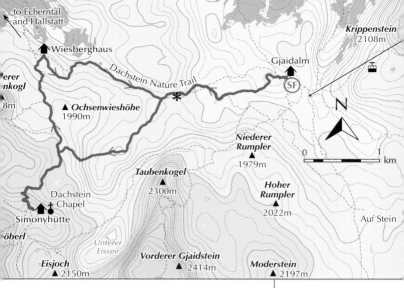

meadow before heading uphill. Go R at the trail junction (the path on the L goes to Oberfeld and Taubenkogel, Walk 26), and keep straight ahead passing another trail to Oberfeld on your L, and ascending through a grassy gully.

> The trail between Gjaidalm and Wiesberghaus is known as the **Dachstein Nature Trail**. A series of small information boards along the route, with text in German and English, describe the geology, glaciers, wildlife and plants found along the trail and surrounding area.

After 1hr from Gjaidalm you round a corner to a **viewpoint** with stupendous views of the Hoher Dachstein and **Hallstätter Glacier**, with Simonyhütte visible near the right-hand edge of the glacier below a reddish area of rock.

Turn L down the trail to Simonyhütte (you'll return along the trail straight ahead, path no. 654 from Wiesberghaus, later), which heads across undulating karst terrain between grassy dolines. Pass a sign to a winter route on your L, and bear R (W), after which the trail goes steeply uphill, rocky and slightly exposed in places, with some sections secured with cables. This leads you up to join the broad, well-built trail coming up from Weisberghaus (path no. 601/no. 650). Turn L onto this trail, which winds across the rock-strewn landscape of the Dachstein plateau, before zigzagging uphill to reach **Simonyhütte**, 45min after joining path no. 601.

> **Simonyhütte** (2203m, open mid-May–late September, food and accommodation) – named after the great Austrian geographer and Alpine researcher Friedrich Simony (1813–96), whose name is synonymous with the exploration of Dachstein and Salzkammergut – sits below the edge of the Hallstätter Glacier, with magnificent views in all directions, and the best *kaiserschmarrn* I've ever tasted. The small Dachstein Chapel (Dachsteinkapelle) dates from 1913 and was built by Matthäus Schlager, one of the master builders

Dachstein Chapel beside Simonyhütte

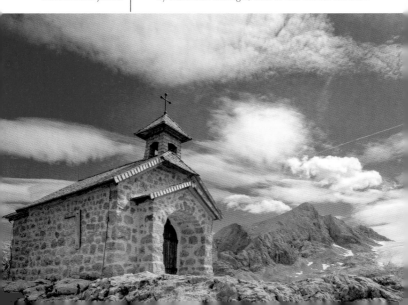

who worked on Linz Cathedral. At 2206m it's the highest church in the Northern Limestone Alps.

Sunrise at Wiesberghaus

Descend from Simonyhütte, retracing your steps but instead of turning R on path no. 650 keep straight ahead on path no. 601. Pass two trails to Ochsenkogel on your L, and a trail to Ochsenwieshöhe on the R, to arrive at **Wiesberghaus**, 1hr from Simonyhütte.

> **Wiesberghaus** (open mid May–late October, food and accommodation) lies on the edge of the Dachstein plateau, above the trail up from Hallstatt through the Echerntal (Walk 24), with breathtaking views of Plassen and the Ochsenkogel and is the author's favourite hut in the Salzkammergut/ Dachstein region.

Take the path SE from Wiesberghaus, contouring the side of the small knoll in front of the hut and winding through a landscape of rocky dells studded with juniper. It's 1hr to the trail junction here, path no. 650 going to the R, and another 1hr to arrive back at **Gjaidalm**.

WALK 26
*Taubenkogel from
Gjaidalm*

Start/finish	Gjaidalm
Distance	7.5km
Ascent/descent	640m
Grade	Difficult
Time	5hr 15min
Terrain	Good, clear paths across rocky karst terrain, with one steep and exposed section secured with cables just below the ridge
Maximum altitude	2300m (Taubenkogel)
Maps	AV (Alpenverein) no. 14 Dachstein (1:25,000); Kompass no. 229 Salzkammergut Sheet 2 (1:50,000)
Refreshments	Gjaidalm (www.gjaid.at/)
Transport	Krippenstein cable car from Obertraun to Gjaidalm

A magnificent, challenging walk to one of the most prominent of the Dachstein high peaks. Taubenkogel forms the northeast buttress of the wall of peaks which enclose one side of the Hallstätter Glacier, sweeping up through the Vorderer, Niederer and Hoher Gjaidstein, to the main Dachstein ridge and the Hoher Dachstein. Its massive cliffs tower over the karst plateau below, but there's a non-technical route up to the summit ridge, with just one short, slightly exposed section.

Follow the path W from in front of Gjaidalm, then turn L on path no. 650 which goes along the edge of a marshy area before heading uphill. Go L at the trail junction (the path on the R goes to Simonyhütte and Wiesberghaus, Walk 25), and ascend on a rocky path, keeping straight ahead past trails to Oberfeld on your L and Wiesberghaus on your R, then another trail to Oberfeld on your L. Cross the shoulder of the **Niederer Rumpler** (1979m), passing an easily missed trail to this peak on your L.

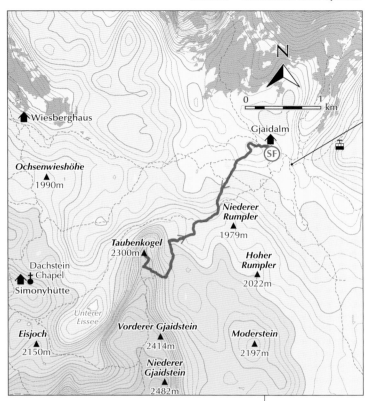

The trail now levels off slightly and goes across a spectacular area of limestone pavement, with the huge northeast buttress of Taubenkogel ahead. Pass a turnoff to the Trägerweg (a more difficult route to Simonyhütte) on the R. Bear L past a large boulder then R up over grassy slopes and onto rock debris. Steep switchbacks are followed by an exposed section secured with cables, which heads diagonally up a narrow ledge to gain a grassy area. Turn R and follow the ridge up to the summit of **Taubenkogel**, 2hr 45min from Gjaidalm.

Exposed section of trail on the route to Taubenkogel

Taubenkogel (2300m) commands breathtaking views across the Hoher Gjaidstein and Hallstätter Glacier to the Hoher Dachstein on one side, and over the sprawling expanse of the Dachstein Plateau (Am Stein) on the other. The small lake below to the southeast is Unterer Eissee – the Hallstätter Glacier descended to this point in 1850.

Descend by the same route to **Gjaidalm** (allow 2hr 30min).

WALK 27

Heilbronner Trail

Start	Krippenstein cable car station
Finish	Gjaidalm cable car station
Distance	9km
Ascent	185m
Descent	470m
Grade	Medium
Time	3hr 15min
Terrain	Broad, rocky 4x4 roads throughout
Maximum altitude	2060m (Krippenstein upper cable car station)
Maps	AV (Alpenverein) no. 14 Dachstein (1:25,000); Kompass no. 229 Salzkammergut Sheet 2 (1:50,000)
Refreshments	Gjaidalm (www.gjaid.at/); Krippenstein cable car station
Transport	Krippenstein cable car

An easy and very popular walk on the edge of the Dachstein plateau, with magnificent views in all directions, oodles of karst features, and a strangely likeable metal shark. It can be walked in either direction, but is described here starting from Krippenstein as that way involves less uphill.

Although it's often called the Heilbronner 'Circuit', the trail is not, in fact, a circuit – and the obvious-looking access road between the cable car stations at the start and end of the route is closed to the public. If you're up for a day trip on the cable car, this won't be an issue. However, if you're staying at Gjaidalm or Wiesberghaus for a few nights and doing day trips from them, you'll have to walk this in reverse then either hike back the same way along the Heilbronner trail, or follow the alternative route over Margschierf (a more difficult trail than the 4x4 road) or path no. 662 via Hirzkarseelein (also more difficult). Alternatively, the most practical solution is to use the Heilbronner Trail to hike out from (or in to) Gjaidalm at the end, or start, of your stay on Dachstein, with full packs. It goes without saying that while it's extremely accessible and very easy, it's still a high mountain plateau which can experience sudden changes in weather conditions at any time of year.

The Heilbronner Trail is widely touted as the most beautiful trail in Salzkammergut. However, while it is a very fine trail and definitely well worth doing, I'd argue that if you only have time for one walk on Dachstein, this isn't the one to do – that accolade goes to the trail to Simonyhütte and Wiesberghaus (Walk 25), which takes you off 4x4 roads altogether and through some of the most breathtaking scenery in Austria.

Before setting off on the trail, it's worth hiking up to the World Heritage Spiral (Welterbespirale) on **Krippenstein summit** and the Pioneer Cross (Pionierkreuz), for enhanced views. These and the popular Five Fingers viewpoint are less than a 15min walk.

There are superlative views of the Hoher Sarstein to the N, rising above the E shore of Hallstätter See.

From in front of the **Krippenstein cable car station**, follow the access road steeply downhill, heading S and passing the ski lift. Follow the 4x4 road SE, passing near an ice cave, and passing a trail on your L to Däumelsee and Däumelkogel (the prominent, nearby peak to the NE) and a trail to Margschierf on the R. ◀

A little over 30min from the Krippenstein cable car station, you arrive at the **Dachstein Shark** (Dachstein Hai), a large hollow metal shark (this was of course, once upon a time, the bottom of the sea) with steps inside, which children (and grown-ups) can climb and look out of its mouth.

The prominent peak roughly ESE is the Hochwildstelle, at 2747m the highest peak entirely within Styria.

Continue past the shark, crossing a saddle between Margschierf and Däumelkogel, and passing a small wooden shelter. Ahead the 4x4 road descends gradually, and there are breathtaking views S, far across the Dachstein plateau to the Schladming Tauern. ◀ Further along, pass the other end of the Margschierf trail on your R. After 1hr 30min from the cable car station you arrive at a junction, with the **Heilbronner Cross** down a short track to your L.

The **Heilbronner Cross** (Heilbronner Kreuz) commemorates the deaths of a school party – three

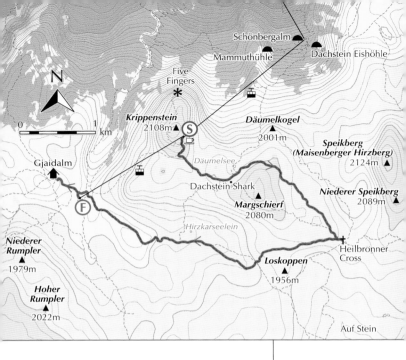

teachers and 10 children – from the German town of Heilbronn, who were caught in a blizzard up here in April 1954.

Return from the junction and follow the 4x4 road W towards Gjaidalm, the huge views continuing to the S, and passing another small wooden shelter on your L and a trail to Loskoppen, also on your L. About 1hr from the Heilbronner Cross, pass a trail on your R to **Hirzkarseelein**, a group of small lakes (there used to be more, but some have dried up) near the abandoned Hirzkaralm. ▶ After 30min beyond the Hirzkarseelein trail, pass the Gjaidalm cable car station on your L. Immediately after this turn L along a 4x4 road (the access road bearing R, leading up to the Krippenstein cable car station, is closed to hikers), going down a steep hill to reach **Gjaidalm** in another 10min.

Allow 20min each way from the main trail if you want to make a detour.

Gjaidalm (1738m, open June–October, food and accommodation) is the kicking-off point for some of the best hiking trails in the area, and has beautiful mountain views from the terrace.

Return to the **Gjaidalm cable car station** (15min) and take the cable car over Krippenstein and down to Obertraun.

WALK 28

Vorderer Gosausee and
Hinterer Gosausee

Start/finish	Gasthof Gosausee
Distance	13.5km
Ascent/descent	260m
Grade	Easy
Time	4hr
Terrain	Easy lakeside and forest walking on broad paths and 4x4 tracks
Maximum altitude	1185m (Hohe Holzmeisteralm)
Maps	AV (Alpenverein) no. 14 Dachstein (1:25,000); Kompass no. 229 Salzkammergut Sheet 2 (1:50,000)
Refreshments	Gasthof Gosausee (www.gasthof-gosausee.at); Hohe Holzmeisteralm at Hinterer Gosausee (tel +43 (0)664 1145 113)
Transport	Bus no. 542 runs from Bad Ischl to Gasthof Gosausee via Bad Goisern (connecting with bus no. 952 to Bad Aussee) and Gosaumühle (connecting with bus no. 543 to Hallstatt and Obertraun), timetables at www.postbus. at
Note	Apart from a small snack and souvenir kiosk, there are no shops at the end of the road, around Gasthof Gosausee – the nearest shops (and the nearest ATM) are back in Gosau.

A short, easy walk alongside the lower and upper Gosau lakes, Vorderer Gosausee and Hinterer Gosausee, surrounded by extraordinarily beautiful scenery including breathtaking views of the Hohe Dachstein and the Gosau Glacier. For a longer, more demanding route there are trails continuing from Hinterer Gosausee up to Ademekhütte. The trail around the lower lake is dotted with a series of installations on the theme of water, entitled Was(ser) leben – great fun for kids, and beginning with one right outside Gasthof Gosausee. Each has a small information card, in German and English.

The walk around Vorderer Gosausee is described here anticlockwise, but you could follow it the opposite way. You might want to base the choice of which side of Vorderer Gosausee you follow for the outward/return journey on the time of day – the cliffs above the north side of the lake are particularly beautiful in the late afternoon/early evening light, and are best viewed from the opposite (south) shore; however, it's at that same time of day that the Hoher Dachstein and Gosau Glacier above the head of the valley, which can only be seen from the north shore, are also at their most beautiful. The trail on the south shore of the lake is the more shaded of the two, the trail on the north shore the more open with views of the Gosaukamm.

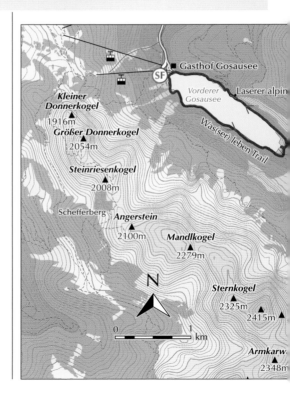

From in front of Gasthof Gosausee, turn right and begin following the broad, level track which encircles **Vorderer Gosausee**. Almost immediately, you pass a small viewing box looking towards the Gosau Glacier, with clear screens to slide in and out which show the relative positions of the glacier at several points in previous centuries, and the dramatic scale of its retreat. Then pass a trail on your right to Gablonzerhütte (see Walk 30). As you continue alongside the lake there are views through the trees to the trail on the opposite shore, including the Laserer alpin Steig, a via ferrata route across the cliffs above and below it.

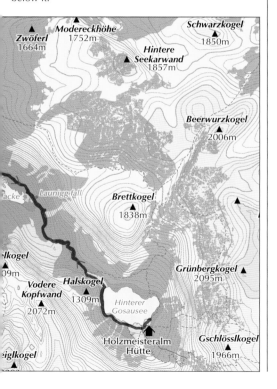

One of the Was(ser) leben objects – a giant funnel

Around halfway along the lake you'll pass what is perhaps the best of the **Was(ser)leben objects** – a giant funnel for listening to the amplified sound of tiny rivulets and drips of water on a mossy rock-face.

As you round the far end of lake, there are a few faint, unmarked paths leading down through the trees on the left to a grassy area beside the lake. However, the ground tends to be a bit boggy here, and the water can be rather stagnant at this end of the lake – meaning that it's not such a great picnic spot as it looks. Hinterer Vordersee is much preferable. There's also an unmarked track on the right which provides a slight shortcut, but there's little to be gained and it's better to just follow the main path.

Turn right onto the broad track coming up from the N side of the lake, which now becomes a 4x4 track and ascends gradually through the forest, passing a farmhouse on the right, and an area with rivulets and streams rushing down from the hillside on your left, where the Launigg spring is located. Shortly after this you reach **Gosaulacke** – a small, shallow pond, in a low-lying clearing on the right of the 4x4 track.

Fed only by the Launigg spring, **Gosaulacke** has been known to dry up in some seasons; however, assuming it's there you'll find a perfect, chocolate-box view of the Hoher Dachstein and Gosau Glacier reflected on its still surface.

Dachstein peaks and Gosau Glacier reflected in Gosaulacke

Beyond Gosaulacke, there's a **waterfall** on the left (Launigg Fall), and the 4x4 track climbs uphill, becoming gradually steeper, with a forest path shadowing the road on the right. On reaching **Hinterer Gosausee** (there's a nice rest spot with a good view on your left as you reach the lake) follow the 4x4 road around the S shore of the lake to reach **Holzmeisteralm Hütte** (1185m, open late May–mid-October, closed Mondays) at the far end, around 2hr from Gasthof Gosausee. The hut has a terrace with fabulous views; there's plenty of scope for a picnic (or a dip) on the grassy banks of the lake below.

Hinterer Gosausee is surrounded by a wall of peaks, with the Brettkogel and Grünbergkogel to the north, the southeast end of the Gosaukamm including Steiglkogel and Sammetkogel to the southwest, and the slopes leading up towards the Gosau Glacier in between.

Beyond Holzmeisteralm Hütte there are two trails leading up to Adamekhütte, which sits perched below the snout of the Gosau Glacier at just under 2200m – the one on the right is the more direct of the two, taking 3hr.

There are spectacular views of the Gosaukamm rising above the opposite shore of the lake – and don't forget to turn around for the breathtaking views back up the valley.

Return to Vorderer Gosausee by the same route, this time following the trail on the N side of the lake. ◄ The trail passes through a gallery below the cliffs, and an information board on the **Laserer alpin Steig**, before merging with the asphalt road and passing a turnoff to Ebenalm (Walk 29), to reach **Gasthof Gosausee** again.

WALK 29
Löckermoos

Start/finish	Gasthof Gosausee
Distance	16km
Ascent/descent	905m
Grade	Medium
Time	5hr 30min
Terrain	Good forest paths, 4x4 tracks and wooden boardwalks over marshland areas
Maximum altitude	1442m (Löckermoos)
Maps	Alpenverein no. 14 Dachstein (1:25,000); Kompass no. 229 Salzkammergut Sheet 2 (1:50,000)
Refreshments	Ebenalm (https://ebenalm-gosau.at/); Triamerhütte in Grubalm
Transport	Bus no. 542 to Gosausee

Löckermoos is an outstandingly beautiful area of blanket bog, high above the Gosautal, with a tiny lake (Löckersee) at its centre. It's one of only five blanket bogs in Austria – two are here in the Gosautal area, the other three are in the Raetian Alps – and it's unusual in that it lies at such a high altitude. The names Löckenmoos, Leckernmoos and Löckernmoos are also used fairly interchangeably.

From Gasthof Gosausee follow the N shore of **Vorderer Gosausee**, and turn L up the unsealed road towards Ebenalm. Go R where the road splits (signposted Ebenalm Waldsteig), after which it rapidly deteriorates into a rough 4x4 track, then bear L, where the route becomes steeper. Go R on a path signposted Ebenalm and Löckermoos, cross a small wooden bridge over a marshy area, then bear R again. After 45min from Gasthof Gosausee, emerge into a grassy clearing with the **Ebenalm** hut in front of you.

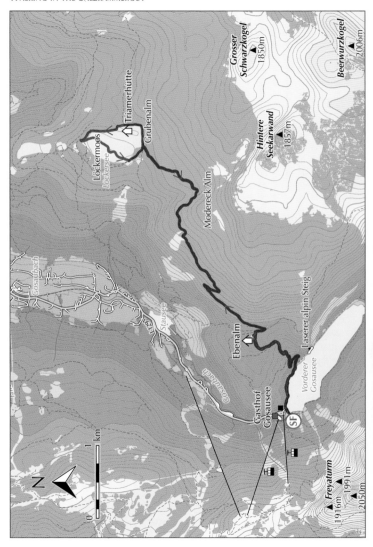

Ebenalm (open June–September, food and accommodation) is a lovely little hut in a rolling clearing, with tasty food.

Pass the hut on your L. ▶ Walk E across pasture and descend to a 4x4 road. Turn R onto this, going uphill slightly, then turn L onto a 4x4 road going N. This ascends gradually, with unsurpassed views over the Gosautal to Gamsfeld (at 2027m, considered to be the highest of the Salzkammergut mountains, when excluding Dachstein and the Totes Gebirge as per the Alpine Club's Classification of the Eastern Alps), and after about 45min a bench to admire the view from. Pass a trail on your R to Seekalm, then 20min from the bench bear R at a junction (signposted Rossalm, Plankesteinalm and Grubalm), after which the 4x4 road contours the hillside above a large clearing. After 10min from the junction turn L to arrive in front of the **Triamerhütte** at Grubalm.

Triamerhütte (open June–September) overlooks Grubalm from just below the 4x4 road. You won't pass it on the way back, so if you want to stop here, now's the time.

The signposting is unclear at this point, marking everything except Löchersee.

The trail across Löckermoos

According to legend, a group of young women used to live here in the rock, emerging only at harvest time when they would go down into the valley to help the farmers.

Follow the path beyond the hut, passing a crevice in the rock on your R known as the Wildfrauenloch. ◄

Beyond the Wildfrauenloch, the trail follows a succession of wooden boardwalks, as it crosses the moorland of Grubalm with its rich plantlife, then becomes a path through woodland. Bear L and follow the path uphill onto **Löckermoos**, then follow wooden boardwalks across this through a sea of blueberry bushes and low dwarf mountain pine, to arrive at the tiny **Löckersee**, 30minutes from Triamerhütte.

Löckersee sits at the centre of the broad expanse of blanket bog that is Löckermoos, its surface reflecting the Gosaukamm. Pollen profiles show Löckermoos to be around 8000 years old. It developed on top of a layer of water-retaining marl, and the peat layer is between 1m and 2m thick, supporting moorland vegetation such as sedges, cottongrass, sundew and peat moss.

Continue SW from Löckersee, descending to reach a small wooden gazebo overlooking meadows and a couple of cottages. Turn L along a 4x4 track to arrive back at the junction with your outgoing route. Turn R and follow the 4x4 road down to Ebenalm (1hr 20min) and the trail down to **Vorderer Gosausee** (another 1hr).

WALK 30
Gosausee to Theodor-Körner Hütte

Start/finish	Gasthof Gosausee
Distance	13km
Ascent/descent	1250m
Grade	Medium
Time	7hr
Terrain	Mountain paths, through forest initially, open rocky slopes later
Maximum altitude	1598m (Törlecksattel)
Maps	AV (Alpenverein) no. 14 Dachstein (1:25,000); Kompass no. 229 Salzkammergut Sheet 2 (1:50,000)
Refreshments	Gablonzerhütte (www.gablonzerhuette.at); Breininghütte; Stuhlalm (https://stuhlalm.at/); Theodor-Körner Hütte (http://koerner-huette.at/)
Transport	Bus no. 542 to Gosausee. It's possible to take the cable car up to Gablonzerhütte (1550m), shaving 1hr 30min each way off the timings given here.

A superb hike over the shoulder of the main Gosaukamm and along their south slopes towards the 2,454m Bischofsmütze (the highest peak in the Gosaukamm), with a couple of very nice huts at the end. One of my favourite walks in Salzkammergut.

This walk can be used as an alternative exit from the area, leaving Salzkammergut/Dachstein on its south edge, providing an onward route back to Salzburg rather than returning via Bad Ischl – which also gives you the chance to visit the ice cave above Werfen (one of the largest in the world), and Burg Hohenwerfen with its spectacular falconry displays.

From Gasthof Gosausee follow the lakeside path W beside **Vorderer Gosausee**, then after around 100m turn R onto a path leading uphill towards Gablonzerhütte. The path heads up steeply through forest, to reach a junction

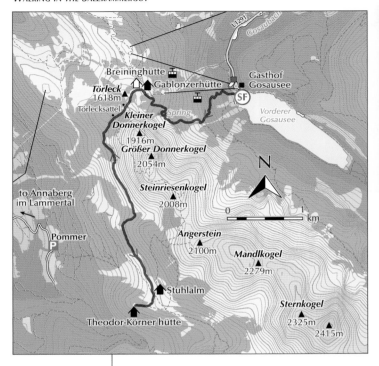

The trail to the L, known as the Steiglweg, crosses scree slopes then climbs over the Steigl Pass to Hofpürglhütte in 3hr 45min, providing a more demanding and exposed route across the Gosaukamm than the one described here.

in 40min, where you turn R. ◄ Continue up over a grassy shoulder above a lone cottage, with increasingly good views back over Vorderer Gosausee. The path steepens again and passes a small **spring**, before levelling off and passing a path leading up from the upper cable car station on the R, to arrive at **Gablonzerhütte**, a little over 1hr 30min from Gasthof Gosausee.

Gablonzerhütte (open May–October, food and accommodation) and **Breininghütte** (open mid May–late October) stand at the start of a trail to Zwieselalm further north.

170

From the trail junction above Gablonzerhütte, follow the path uphill past **Breininghütte**, signposted to the Großer Donnerkogel, ascending over the S slopes of **Törleck** (1618m) to reach the **Northeast Törlecksattel** (1598m), 20min from Gablonzerhütte.

Crossing the Northeast Törlecksattel

> The **Northeast Törlecksattel** is the slightly higher of the two Törleck saddles – the **West Törlecksattel**, slightly further along the route, is 1576m. There are phenomenal views down the length of Vorderer Gosausee to the Gosau Glacier, and the route to Ebenalm and Löckermoos (Walk 27) can be seen above the north shore of the lake. A popular via ferrata route to the Großer Donnerkogel (2054m) ascends on your left, while to the west the view stretches to the Tennegebirge.

Go through a turnstile and follow the grassy path SW, downhill slightly then over the **West Törlecksattel** and keeping straight ahead past a trail on the L to the Großer Donnerkogel. ▸ After going through forest for a while, the path crosses open, rocky slopes and scree, mildly exposed in places. After 1hr 30min from the Northeast Törlecksattel go L along a 4x4 road to arrive in another 15min at **Stuhlalm**.

This is a hiking route not a climbing route, but still slightly exposed in places – it's 1hr 15min to the top if you want to make a detour.

Stuhlalm (1467m, open daily mid May–October, food and accommodation) is a lovely welcoming hut which sits on open grassy slopes below the jagged line of the Gosaukamm, culminating to the southeast in the soaring bulk of the Bischofsmütze (2430m) which you need to continue a bit further southeast to get a proper view of – though the view in the opposite direction to the Tennegebirge more than makes up for this small detail.

The unsealed road in front of the hut goes down in long switchbacks to Annaberg im Lammertal (note that timings to Annaberg im Lammertal on signs typically refer to the car park at Pommer not to Annaberg im Lammertal itself – more accurately, it's 1hr 30min to the car park at Pommer, and another 7km or so on asphalt road to the bus stop in Annaberg im Lammertal).

Continue past Stuhlalm following the 4x4 road as it turns S, and bear R to reach **Theodor-Körner Hütte** in under 10min.

Theodor-Körner Hütte (1454m, open 1 June–mid October, food and accommodation) sits in a wonderful setting on the edge of the trees, with a nice terrace and jaw-dropping views of the Bischofsmütze.

Return to **Gasthof Gosausee** by the same route (allow at least 3hr).

Walk	Start	Distance	Ascent/descent	Grade	Time	Page
1	Fuschl am See	11.5km	390m	Easy	3hr	47
2	Fuschl am See	6.5km	485m	Easy	2hr 15min	50
3	Fuschl am See	10km	745m	Easy–medium	4hr 30min	52
4	St Gilgen	5km	455m	Easy–medium	2hr 30min	55
5	Zwölferhorn	8.5km	285m/1185m	Easy	3hr 40min	58
6	St Wolfgang	9km	495m/495m	Easy	2hr 30min	62
7	Schafbergbahn	10km	130m/1360m	Medium	3hr 20min	66
8	St Lorenz	12km	950m	Medium–difficult	5hr	71
9	Gmunden	13.5km	780m/780m	Easy–medium	5hr	78
10	Vorderer Langbathsee	7km	80m	Easy	2hr	82
11	Feuerkogel Seilbahn	7.5km	440m	Medium	3hr 30min	84
12	Feuerkogel Seilbahn	9km	555m	Medium	5hr	89
13	Offensee	14km	1145m	Medium	6hr	93
14	Katrin Seilbahn	7.5km	340m/1265m	Easy–medium	4hr 30min	97
15	Bad Goisern	7km	500m/515m	Easy	2hr 40min	101
16	Altaussee	7.5km	335m	Easy	2hr 30min	109
17	Altaussee	15km	1290m	Difficult	6hr 30min	112

Walk	Start	Distance	Ascent/descent	Grade	Time	Page
18	Altaussee	16km	1245m	Medium–difficult	8hr 45min	116
19	Altaussee	10.5km	535m	Medium	4hr 20min	119
20	Grundlsee	15.5km	630m/630m	Medium	6hr	122
21	Gößl	12.5km	725m	Medium	4hr 30min	128
22	Gößl	20km	1240m	Medium–difficult	7hr	131
23	Obersee	5km	95m/95m	Easy	2hr	139
24	Hallstatt Lahn	15km	1840m/570m	Medium	7hr 15min	143
25	Gjaidalm	13.5km	800m	Medium	6hr	148
26	Gjaidalm	7.5km	640m	Difficult	5hr 15min	152
27	Krippenstein	9km	185m/470m	Medium	3hr 15min	155
28	Gasthof Gosausee	13.5km	260m	Easy	4hr	159
29	Gasthof Gosausee	16km	905m	Medium	5hr 30min	165
30	Gasthof Gosausee	13km	1250m	Medium	7hr	169

APPENDIX B

Gateway cities: Salzburg and Linz

Salzburg

Salzburg's exceptionally beautiful old town centre, on the banks of the River Salzach, is one of the most cohesive and best preserved examples of Baroque architecture anywhere, and is a UNESCO World Heritage Site. While staying in the city of Mozart don't miss visiting the Mozart Birth House (https://mozarteum.at/en/museums/mozarts-birth place/), the Hohensalzburg Fortress (the largest fully preserved castle in central Europe www.salzburg-burgen.at/en/hohensalzburg-castle/), Mirabell Palace and Gardens (of the 'Do-Re-Mi' scene of *The Sound of Music* fame), the opulent DomQuartier (www. domquartier.at/), and the Museum of Modern Art (www.museumdermoderne.at/en/) which has around 55,000 works from the 19th century to the present day.

Arriving

If you're arriving into Salzburg Hauptbahnhof by train, simply walk out of the main entrance of the station onto Sudtirolplatz – bus no. 150 to Bad Ischl departs from bus stop F; you can buy tickets from the driver. If you've flown into Salzburg Airport (www.salzburg-airport.com/en/), bus no. 2 departs every 10–20min from just across the car park outside Arrivals and goes to the Hauptbahnhof (journey time 20min, timetables at www.salzburg-ag.at and click on Verkehr then Fahrplan); buy tickets from the machine by the bus stop (travelling back to the airport by bus no. 2: there are ticket machines at the bus station outside the Hauptbahnhof, and there's a ticket office downstairs). For information on Salzburg's S-Bahn network see www.oebb.at.

Recommended accommodation

Hotel Meininger (18–20 Fürbergstraße, www.meininger-hotels.com; take the S-Bahn from the Hauptbahnhoff to Salzburg Gnigl) is the best value place to stay in Salzburg; Hotel & Villa Auersperg (61 Auerspergstraße, www.auersperg.at) is excellent, close to Linzergasse and the old city centre.

Salzburg Tourist Office

Offices at the Hauptbahnhof (Südtiroler Platz 1) and on Mozartplatz (Mozartplatz 5) www.salzburg.info/en/.The Salzburg Card gives free admission to museums and on public transport within the city and is available for durations of 24hr, 48hr and more.

Linz

Linz has some excellent museums, galleries and concert halls, including the Lentos Kunstmuseum (https://lentos.at/), an outstanding collection of modern and contemporary art located in an iconic building on the bank of the Danube, the Ars Electronica Centre (https://ars.electronica.art/), and the Schlossmuseum (www.landesmuseum.at/en/location/schlossmuseum-linz.html), as well as an extraordinary collection of street art on the sides of giant warehouses at the harbour. Linz's Mariendom (New Cathedral) is the largest church in Austria.

Arriving

Linz Hauptbahnhof is located a 15min walk south of the old town. If you've flown into Linz Airport (www.linz-airport.com/), bus no. 601 runs to the Hauptbahnhof every 30–60min (journey time around 20min, timetables at www.ooevv.at where the airport is listed as Flughafen Linz Terminal – or more usefully, just see the public transport information on www.linz-airport.com). If you're travelling back to the airport on bus no. 601, note that the airport is not the final stop – the bus continues to Traun Trauner Kreuzung. You can also reach the airport by train from either Linz or Wels – take a train to Hörsching, where a shuttle bus takes passengers on to the airport itself. For onward travel to Salzkammergut, take a train from Linz Hauptbahnhof to Attnang-Puchheim and change there onto the train to Ebensee/Bad Ischl/Obertraun.

Recommended accommodation

Hotel Wolfinger (Hauptplatz 19, www.hotelwolfinger.at) is a historic inn on the main square.

Linz Tourist Office

Office on the main square (Hauptplatz 1) www.linztourismus.at. The Linz Card gives free admission into the main museums and galleries and covers free public transport within the city centre, and is available in durations of 24hr and 3 days www.linztourismus.at/en/leisure/plan-a-trip/linzcard/.

APPENDIX C
Further reading

Natural history
Klaas-Douwe B Dijkstra and Richard Lewington, *Field Guide to the Dragonflies of Britain and Europe* (British Wildlife Publishing, 2006)
Ansgar Hoppe, *Flowers of the Alps* (Pelagic Publishing, 2013)
E Nicolas, Arnold and Denys W Ovenden, *Reptiles and Amphibians of Europe* (Princeton Field Guides, 2002)
Oleg Polunin, *The Concise Flowers of Europe* (Oxford, 1972)
Gillian Price, *Alpine Flowers* (Cicerone, 2014)
Lars Svensson, Killian Mullarney, Dan Zetterström and Peter J Grant, *Birds of Europe* (Princeton University Press, 2010), also available as *Collins' Bird Guide* (Harper Collins, 2010)
Tom Tolman and Richard Lewington, *Collins Butterfly Guide* (Collins, 2009)

History
Steve Beller, *A Concise History of Austria* (Cambridge, 2007)
Karina Gromer, *Textiles from Hallstatt* (Archaeolingua, 2013)
Pieter M Judson, *The Habsburg Empire: A New History* (Harvard, 2016)
Anton Kern (ed), *Kingdom of Salt: 7000 Years of Hallstatt* (Natural History Museum Vienna, 2009)
Martyn Rady, *The Habsburg Empire: A Very Short Introduction* (Oxford, 2017)

Language
Teach Yourself German (Teach Yourself, 2007)
Collins Easy Learning – Complete German (Collins, 2016)
Collins Gem German Phrasebook and Dictionary (Collins, 2016)

APPENDIX D
English–German glossary

The following, brief language guide and glossary covers some basic phrases and useful words in German. Words that are colloquially used in Austria are marked '(Aus)'.

Pronunciation

Note that several letters or combinations of letters are pronounced differently in German to how they would be in English:

ä – pronounced similar to the 'ai' in hair
ö – pronounced similar to the 'ur' in Arthur
ü – pronounced similar to the 'ue' sound in due
ch – after a vowel, pronounced as the 'ch' in loch
ai – pronounced as the 'ie' in lie
ie – pronounced as the 'ee' in keep
j – pronounced as the 'y' in yes
qu – pronounced 'kv'
sch – pronounced as the 'sh' in shine
ß – (also written as 'ss'), pronounced 'ss'
th – pronounced as the 't' in tea
v – pronounced as the 'f' in feel
w – pronounced as the 'v' in vet

Greetings, introductions and basic phrases

There are several informal greetings, not used in standard German, which you will hear frequently in Salzkammergut or elsewhere in Austria: Grüß Gott! (literally, 'May God greet you'); Servus! (slightly less formal than Grüß Gott!); and Grüß dich! Hallo! are also used widely.

English	German
Hello/Good day (formal)	Guten Tag
Good morning	Guten Morgen
Good evening	Guten Abend
Goodbye	Auf Wiedersehen
Bye! (informal)	Tschüss! or Pfiat di! (Aus)
Yes	Ja
No	Nein
Please	Bitte
Thank you (very much)	Danke (schön)

English	German
You're welcome (in response to thank you)	Bitte
Excuse me	Entschuldigung
Sorry!	Tut mir leid!
Do you speak English?	Sprechen Sie Englisch?
I don't speak German	Ich spreche kein Deutsch
How are you? (formal)	Wie geht es Ihnen?
Fine, thank you	Danke, gut
Where are you from?	Woher kommen Sie?
Cheers! (as a toast)	Prost!
Bon appetite	Guten Appetit or more colloquially, Mahlzeit
Where is…?	Wo ist…?
How do I get to…?	Wie komme ich zum…?
Where is the toilet?	Wo ist die Toilette?
How much does it cost?	Wieviel kostet das?
Can I have the bill, please?	Die Rechnung, bitte.

General vocabulary

English	German
bad	schlecht
big	gross
closed	geschlossen
difficult	schwer
easy	leicht
entrance	Eingang
exit	Ausgang
good	gut
open	geöffnet
small	klein
with	mit
without	ohne

Directions

English	German
here/there	hier/dort
high/low	hohe/niedrig
hiking map	Wanderkarte
left/right	links/recht
near/far	nah/weit
north/south/east/west	Nord/Süd/Ost/West
over/under	über/unter
(go) straight ahead	geradeaus (gehen)

Landscape

English	German
cairn	Steinpyramide
cave	Höhle
cycle path	Radweg
forest	Wald
glacier	Gletscher
gorge	Schlucht
lake	See

English	German
marsh	Moor
mountain	Berg
mountain hut	Hütte
nature reserve	Naturschutzgebiet
pass	Sattel
path	Steig/Weg
peak	Spitze
ridge	Rücken
river	Fluss
rocky	felsig
saddle	Sattel
scree	Geröll
sinkhole	Schacht
spring	Quelle
steep	steil
stone	Stein
stream	Bach
summit	Höhepunkt
4x4 track	Karrenweg
valley	Tal
via ferrata	Klettersteig
water	Wasser
waterfall	Wasserfall

Weather

English	German
cloudy	bewölkt
cold	kalt
hail	Hagel
hot	heiß
ice	Eis
lightning	Blitz
mist	Nebel
rain	Regen
sun	Sonne

English	German
sunny	sonnig
snow	Schnee
storm/ thunderstorm	Gewitter
thunder	Donner
warm	warm
weather	Wetter
weather forecast	Wettervorhersage
wind	Wind

Plants and animals

English	German
beech	Buche
bird	Vogel
butterfly	Schmetterling
chamois	Gams
common adder	Kreuzotter or Höllenotter
deer	Hirsch
eagle	Adler
flower	Blume
fox	Fuchs
larch	Lärche
mountain pine	Latschenkiefern
tree	Baum
snake	Schlange

Hiking equipment

English	German
compass	Kompass
hiking boots	Wanderstiefel
hiking map	Wanderkarte
hiking poles	Trekkingstöcke
map	Karte
rucksack	Rucksack

English	German
sleeping bag	Schlafsack
sleeping bag liner	Hüttenschlafsack

Transport

English	German
airport	Flughafen
arrivals/departures	Ankunft/Abfahrt
bus	Bus
bus station	Busbahnhof
bus stop	Haltestelle
cable car	Seilbahn
ferry	Fähre
platform	Bahnsteig
railway	Bahn
railway station	Bahnhof
railway station (Main)	Hauptbahnhof (abbreviated Hbf)
single ticket/return ticket	einfache Fahrt/ Hin- und Rückfahrt (or say hin und zurück)
taxi	Taxi
ticket	Fahrkarte
ticket office	Fahrkartenschalter
timetable	Fahrplan
train	Zug

Accommodation

English	German
(AAC) members/ non-members	Mitglieder/ Nicht-Mitglieder
bathroom	Badezimmer
bed	Bett
dormitory	Matratzenlager
half board	Halbpension
hostel	Hostel
hotel	Hotel

English	German
mountain hut	Hütte
guesthouse	Pension
room	Zimmer
shared room	Mehrbettzimmer
single room/ double room	Einzelzimmer/ Doppelzimmer
sheet sleeping bag	Hüttenschlafsack

Food and restaurants (also see menu reader in Introduction)

English	German
I'm allergic to…	Ich bin allergisch auf…
I'm vegetarian	Ich bin Vegetarier/ Vegetarierin (m/f)
beef	Rindfleisch
beer	Bier
bread	Brot
bread roll	Semmel
breakfast	Frühstück
char (fish)	Saibling
cheese	Käse
chicken	Hühnchen
coffee	Kaffee
dinner	Abendessen
dumpling	Knödel
fish	Fisch
fruit	Obst
gluten-free	glutenfrei
inn/tavern	Gasthaus
lunch	Mittagessen
meat	Fleisch
menu	Speisekarte
mushrooms	Pilze
pork	Schweinefleisch
potatoes	Kartoffeln or Erdäpfel (Aus)

181

English	German
restaurant	Restaurant
salad	Salat
sausage	Wurst
soup	Suppe
tea	Tee
trout	Forelle
vegetables	Gemüse
vegetarian	Vegetarisch
venison	Rehfleisch
wine	Wein

In town

English	German
castle	Schloss/Burg
cathedral	Dom
centre	Zentrum
chapel	Kapelle
church	Kirche
monastery	Kloster
museum	Museum
pharmacy	Apotheke
post office	Postamt
ruins	Ruine
square	Platz
street	Straße
supermarket	Supermarkt
town/city	Stadt
village	Dorf

Money

English	German
ATM	Automat
bank	Bank
credit card	Kreditkarte

English	German
currency exchange office	Wechselstube
money	Geld

Timings

English	German
day	Tag
hour	Stunde
in the morning	am Morgen
in the evening	Abends
minute	Minute
month	Monat
today	heute
tomorrow	morgen
week	Woche
yesterday	gestern

Dangers and emergencies

English	German
accident	Unfall
ambulance	Krankenwagen
blood	Blut
broken (bone)	gebrochen
Danger!	Achtung!
doctor	Arzt
Help!	Hilfe!
hospital	Krankenhaus
police	Polizei

APPENDIX E
Useful contacts

Embassies
British Embassy (Vienna)
Jauresgasse 12
1030 Vienna
tel +43 (0)1 716 130
www.gov.uk/world/organisations/
british-embassy-vienna

Embassy of Ireland (Vienna)
Rotenturmstraße 16–18
A-1010 Vienna
tel +43 (0)1 715 4246
ww.dfa.ie/irish-embassy/austria/

French Embassy (Vienna)
Technikerstr. 2
1040 Vienna
tel +43 (0)1 502 750
https://at.ambafrance.org

Embassy of the Netherlands (Vienna)
Opernring 5 (7. Stock)
1010 Vienna
tel +43 (0)1 589 39
www.niederlandeweltweit.nl/laender/
osterreich

US Embassy (Vienna)
Boltzmanngasse 16
1090 Vienna
tel +43 (0)1 313 390
https://at.usembassy.gov

Local, regional and national tourist offices
Ausseerland Tourist Office
https://ausseerland.salzkammergut.at

Austrian National Tourist Office
www.austria.info

Bad Ischl Tourist Office
https://badischl.salzkammergut.at

Dachstein-Salzkammergut Tourist Office
https://dachstein.salzkammergut.at

Fuschlsee Tourist Office
https://fuschlsee.salzkammergut.at

Mondsee-Irrsee Tourist Office
https://mondsee.salzkammergut.at

Salzkammergut Tourismus
www.salzkammergut.at

Traunsee-Almtal Tourist Office
https://traunsee-almtal.salzkammergut.at

Wolfgangsee Tourismus
https://wolfgangsee.salzkammergut.at

Dachstein Glacier
www.dachsteingletscher.info

Hiking
Austrian Alpine Club (Österreichischer
Alpenverein – OAV) www.alpenverein.at/
portal/index.php

Maps
The Map Shop
www.themapshop.co.uk

Stanfords
www.stanfords.co.uk

Natural history
Amphibians and Reptiles of Europe
www.herpetology.eu

euroButterflies
www.eurobutterflies.com

Moths and Butterflies of Europe
https://leps.it

Public transport
Austrian Railways
www.oebb.at/en/

Postbus
www.postbus.at

Salzburg Verkehr
https://salzburg-verkehr.at

Verbund Linie
www.verbundlinie.at

Seat61
www.seat61.com

Eco Passenger
http://ecopassenger.hafas.de

Explore the world with Cicerone

walking • trekking • mountaineering • climbing • mountain biking • cycling • via ferratas • scrambling • trail running • skills and techniques

For over 50 years, Cicerone have built up an outstanding collection of nearly 400 guides, inspiring all sorts of amazing experiences.

www.cicerone.co.uk – where adventures begin

- Our **website** is a treasure-trove for every outdoor adventurer. You can buy books or read inspiring articles and trip reports, get technical advice, check for updates, and view videos, photographs and mapping for routes and treks.

- **Register this book** or any other Cicerone guide in your member's library on our website and you can choose to automatically access updates and GPX files for your books, if available.

- Our **fortnightly newsletters** will update you on new publications and articles and keep you informed of other news and events. You can also follow us on Facebook, Twitter and Instagram.

We hope you have enjoyed using this guidebook. If you have any comments you would like to share, please contact us using the form on our website or via email, so that we can provide the best experience for future customers.

CICERONE

Juniper House, Murley Moss Business Village, Oxenholme Road, Kendal LA9 7RL

✉ info@cicerone.co.uk   cicerone.co.uk 🅕🅣🅘